TAROT
in the
SPIRIT
of ZEN

ALSO BY OSHO

TAROT
in the
SPIRIT
of ZEN

The Game of Life

OSHO

St. Martin's Griffin
New York

OSHO ® is a registered trademark of Osho International Foundation, used under license

www.stmartins.com

Design by Kathryn Parise

ISBN 0-312-31767-0

10   9   8   7

CONTENTS

THE SUIT OF RAINBOWS
(DISKS, PENTACLES)

FOREWORD

In 1995, St. Martin's Press published the revolutionary Osho Zen Tarot for the first time. This extraordinarily beautiful and accessible Tarot deck has since become a modern classic, and its uniquely contemporary message has been translated into more than a dozen languages.

Tarot in the Spirit of Zen is a handbook designed to broaden and deepen the understanding of those who use the Osho Zen Tarot. This audience of readers will understand immediately how to use this book as a valuable supplement to the handbook they already have, which comes packaged together with cards. We know they will welcome its publication with as much enjoyment as we have had in selecting and compiling the materials for publication.

Users of other, more traditional tarots, like the Crowley and Rider-Waite decks, will also find this book to be a valuable addition to their libraries. For these readers, we have provided a table of correspondences at the back of the book. The book is organized into chapters corresponding to the seventy-eight cards in a standard tarot deck. In the table, you will find the names of each chapter in the book and the references to corresponding cards in both the Crowley and Rider-Waite decks.

Newcomers to the tarot will particularly enjoy the tear-out "mini-cards" bound into the back of the book, representing the Major Arcana cards of the Osho Zen Tarot. In the tarot system these cards represent the major transformation points that recur throughout the cycle of a life. The cards correspond to Chapters 0 (The Fool) through XXI (Completion) in the text.

Unlike traditional tarot, with its focus on predicting future events, the Zen approach to tarot aims to bring clarity and insight to the present moment. This is based on the understanding that life can seem random and accidental only if we remain unaware and asleep through it. Neither is life something controlled and directed by "fate"—it is a constantly unfolding process of opportunities for learning and growth. Zen insists that we take individual responsibility for this learning and growth, and the first step in taking that responsibility is to have the courage to look at our present realities without judgment or condemnation. In other words, there are no "evil forces" in Zen—only awareness or unawareness, awakening or sleep.

For more about what distinguishes the Zen approach to tarot from more traditional approaches, be sure to read the Introduction chapter. And most of all . . . enjoy the game.

Sarito Carol Neiman
OSHO INTERNATIONAL

EPIGRAPH

Life is the game of games, the ultimate game. It has tremendous meaning if you take it as a game and you don't become serious about it. If
you remain simple and innocent, the game is going to impart many
things to you.

All these games are like classes at a university. You pass through
each class; you learn something. Then you move into another class. So
this game of life has to be played very skillfully. If you are not skillful,
you will miss much that is valuable. To be skillful means to be aware.
Bring more awareness into each act of your life, into each step of your
being.

—Osho

INTRODUCTION

On Predicting the Future

*Freedom can exist only if the future is open. But about an
open future there is no possibility of prediction. The man
who was so beautiful today may commit a murder tomorrow.
Tomorrow is open.*

One thing that is very fundamental has to be remembered, and that is
that whenever we are doing anything—astrology, future prediction,
horoscope readings, palmistry, the I-Ching, tarot—anything that is
concerned with the future, it is basically a reading of the unconscious
of the person. It has nothing much to do with the future. It has more
to do with the past, but because the future is created by the past, it is
relevant to the future, too. Because people live like mechanical things,
the prediction is possible. If you know the past of the person, unless
the person is a buddha, you will be able to predict his future because
he is going to repeat it. If he has been an angry person in the past, he
is carrying the tendency to be angry; that tendency will have effects in
the future.

Ordinarily, an unconscious being goes on repeating his past again and again. It is a wheel-like phenomenon, he repeats it; he cannot do anything else. He cannot bring any new thing into his life, he cannot have a breakthrough. That's why all these sciences work. If people are more aware, more alert, they won't work.

You cannot read the horoscope of a buddha, or read his hand, because he is so free of the past and he is so empty in the present that there is nothing to read!

※

There has been a great misunderstanding between life and time. Time is thought to consist of three tenses: past, present, future—which is wrong. Time consists only of past and future. It is life that consists of the present.

So those who want to live, for them there is no other way than to live this moment. Only the present is existential. The past is simply a collection of memories, and the future is nothing but your imaginations, your dreams.

Reality is here, now. Those who want just to think about life, about living, about love—for them, past and future are perfectly beautiful because they give infinite scope. They can decorate their past, make it as beautiful as they like—although they never lived it; when it was present they were not there. These are just shadows, reflections. They were continuously running, and while running they have seen a few things. They think they have lived. But in the past, only death is the reality, not life. In the future also, only death is the reality, not life.

Those who have missed living in the past—automatically, to substitute for the gap—start dreaming about the future. Their future is only a projection out of the past. Whatever they have missed in the past, they are hoping for in the future; and between the two non-existences is the small, existent moment that is life.

For those who want to live, not to think about it; to love, not to think about it; to be, not to philosophize about it—there is no other alternative. Drink the juices of the present moment, squeeze it totally because it is not going to come back again. Once gone, it is gone forever.

But because of the misunderstanding, which has been almost as old as man—and all the cultures have joined in it—people have made the present part of time. And the present has nothing to do with time. If you are just here in this moment, there is no time. There is immense silence, stillness, no movement; nothing is passing, everything has come to a sudden stop.

The present gives you the opportunity to dive deep into the water of life, or to fly high into the sky of life. But on both sides there are dangers—past and future are the most dangerous words in human language. Between past and future, living in the present is almost like walking on a tightrope—on both sides there is danger. But once you have tasted the juice of the present, you don't care about dangers. Once you are in tune with life, then nothing matters. And to me, life is all there is.

You can call it "God," but that is not a good name because religions have contaminated it. You can call it "existence," which is beautiful. But what you call it is not of any consequence. The understanding should be clear that you have only one moment in your hands—the real moment. And again and again you will get that real moment. Either you live it or you leave it unlived.

Most people simply drag themselves from the cradle to the grave without living at all. I have heard a Sufi story about a man, when he died, who suddenly realized, "My God, I was alive." Only death, as a contrast, made him aware that for seventy years he had been alive. But life itself had not enriched him.

It is not the fault of life. It is our misunderstanding.

Watchfulness will give you life without even thinking about it, because watchfulness can only be in the present. You can witness only the present. Live totally and live intensely, so that each moment becomes golden, and your whole life becomes a series of golden moments.

THE MAJOR ARCANA

0. The Fool

Life is trial and error; one has to learn through errors.

A fool falls out of a sixth-story window. He is lying on the ground with a big crowd around him. A cop walks over and says, "What happened?" The fool says, "I don't know. I just got here."

In the old days all great emperors always had one fool in their court. They had many wise men, counselors, ministers and prime ministers, but always one fool. All the intelligent and wise emperors all over the world, in the East and the West, had a court joker, a fool. Why? Because there are things so-called wise men will not be able to understand, that only a foolish man can understand. Because the so-called wise are so foolish that their cunningness and cleverness closes their minds.

A fool is simple—and was needed, because many times the so-called wise would not say something because they were afraid of the emperor. A fool is not afraid of anybody else. He will speak, whatever the consequences. A fool is a man who will not think of the consequences.

Let me explain to you how many types of fools there are.

The first: one who knows not, and knows not that he knows not . . . the simple fool. Then the second: one who knows not but thinks that he knows . . . the complex fool, the learned fool. And the third: one who knows that he knows not—the blessed fool.

Everybody is born as a simple fool—that is the meaning of "simpleton." Every child is a simple fool. He knows not that he knows not. He has not yet become aware of the possibility of knowing. That is the Christian parable of Adam and Eve. God said to them, "Don't eat the fruit of the tree of knowledge." Before that accident of eating the fruit of the tree of knowledge, they were simple fools. They knew nothing. Of course, they were tremendously happy because when you know not, it is difficult to be unhappy. Unhappiness needs a little training, a little efficiency is needed to create it; unhappiness needs a little technology. You cannot create hell without knowledge. How can you create hell without knowledge?

Adam and Eve were like small children. Every time a child is born, an Adam is born. And he lives for a few years—at the most four years, and that time is becoming less and less every day. He lives in paradise because he knows not how to create misery. He trusts life; he enjoys small things—pebbles on the shore, or seashells. He gathers them as if he has found a treasure. Ordinary colored stones look like Kohinoors. Everything fascinates him—the dewdrops in the morning sun, the stars in the night, the moon, the flowers, the butterflies, everything is a sheer fascination.

But then, by and by, he starts knowing: a butterfly is just a butterfly. A flower is just a flower. There is nothing much in it. He starts knowing the names: this is a rose and that is a lily and that is a marigold and this is a lotus. And by and by those names become barriers. The more he knows, the more he is cut off from life as such. He becomes "heady." Now he lives through the head, not through his totality.

That is the meaning of the fall. He has eaten of the tree of knowledge. Every child has to eat of the tree of knowledge.

Every child is so simple that he has to become complex—that is part of the growth. So every child moves from simple foolishness toward complex foolishness. There are different degrees of complex foolishness—a few people only graduate from high school, a few people become college graduates, a few become doctors and Ph.D.s—there are degrees. But every child has to taste something of knowledge because the temptation to know is great. Anything that is standing there unknown becomes dangerous, a danger. It has to be known because with knowledge we will be able to cope with it. Without knowledge, how are we going to cope with it? So every child is bound to become knowledgeable.

So the first type of fool, out of necessity, has to become the second type of fool. But from the second, the third may happen or may not happen; there is no necessity. The third is possible only when the second type of foolishness has become a great burden—one has carried knowledge too much, to the extreme. One has become just the head and has lost all sensitivity, all awareness, all livingness; one has become just theories and scriptures and dogmas and words and words whirling around in the mind. One day, if the person is aware, he has to drop all that. Then he becomes the third type of fool—the blessed fool.

Then he attains to a second childhood; again he is a child.

Remember Jesus' saying, "In my kingdom of God only those who are like small children will be welcomed." But remember, he says *like* small children, he does not say "small children." Small children cannot enter; they have to pass through the ways of the world, they have to be poisoned in the world and then they have to clean themselves. That experience is a must. So he does not say "small children," he says those who are *like* small children. That word *like* is very significant. It means those who are *not* children, and yet are *like* children.

Children are saints, but their sainthood is only because they have not yet experienced the temptations of sin. Their saintliness is very simple. It has not much value because they have not earned it, they have not worked for it; they have not yet been tempted to go against it. The temptations are coming sooner or later. A thousand and one temptations will be there, and the child will be pulled in many directions. And I am not saying that he should not go in those directions. If he inhibits himself, represses himself from going, he will remain always the first type of fool. He will simply remain ignorant. His ignorance will be nothing but a repression, it will not be an unburdening.

First he has to attain knowledge, first he has to sin, and only after sin and knowledge and disobeying and going into the wilderness of the world, going astray, living his own life of the ego, will he become capable one day to drop it all.

Not everybody will drop it all. All children move from the first foolishness to the second, but from the second only a few blessed ones move to the third—hence they are called blessed fools.

The blessed fool is the greatest possibility of understanding because the blessed fool has come to know that knowledge is futile. He has come to know that all knowledge is a barrier to knowing. Knowledge is a barrier to knowing, so he drops knowledge and becomes a pure knower. He simply attains to clarity of vision. His eyes are empty of theories and thoughts. His mind is no longer a mind; his mind is just intelligence, pure intelligence. His mind is no longer cluttered with junk; his mind is no longer cluttered with borrowed knowledge. He is simply aware. He is a flame of awareness.

I. Existence

We are part of existence, we are not separate. Even if we want to be separate, we cannot be. . . . And the more you are together with existence, the more alive you are.

Live totally, live intensely, because the deeper your living is the more you are in contact with existence. You are born of it; every moment you are renewed, rejuvenated, resurrected by each of your breaths, by each of your heartbeats—existence is taking care of you.

Just as you start watching your breathing, you start seeing a great phenomenon—that through your breath, you are continuously connected with existence. Uninterruptedly—there is no holiday. Whether you are awake or asleep, existence goes on pouring life into you, and taking out all that is dead.

When I say, "Existence takes care," I am not talking philosophy. Philosophy is mostly nonsense. I am simply talking an actual fact. And if you become consciously aware of it, this creates a great trust in you. My saying, "Existence takes care," is meant to trigger a consciousness that can bring the beauty of trusting in existence.

There is no need to believe in a hypothetical God, and there is no need to have faith in a messiah, in a savior; these are all childish desires to have some father figure who takes care of you. And they are all hypothetical. There has not been any savior in the world.

Existence is enough unto itself. Inquire into your relationship with existence, and out of that inquiry trust arises—not belief, not faith. Trust has a beauty because it is your experience. Trust will help you to relax because the whole existence is taking care—there is no need to be worried and to be concerned.

The whole of existence is full of rejoicing; you just need to open your windows. Your darkness is your own creation, your alienation is your own creation; otherwise you are not a stranger to yourself. You are not a stranger to the trees, to the rivers, to the mountains.

It is our existence; we are part of it.

Our heartbeat is part of the universal heartbeat.

And it is not a dead universe; it is immensely intelligent, conscious, sensitive. It is divine in its every dimension. But you have to learn to participate in the dance.

II. Inner Voice

We unnecessarily go on seeking advice from the outside when existence is ready to speak to us from the innermost core of our being. It is already there, but we never listen to that still, small voice.

None of the voices inside you come from the inner self. All voices come from the mind. When all voices are absent, the inner self inspires you in silence toward a certain action, a certain direction. It does not come in words—it is just a silent indication. Otherwise it would be absolutely impossible to find out which is the voice of the inner self.

It is easy because *no* voice is of the inner self. So when all voices have died down and there is utter silence, the inner self is capable of taking your hand and moving you. That is the moment to be in a let-go, and allow it to take you wherever it takes you.

In language we have to use words that do not apply to the inner reality—for example, the "inner voice." There is no voice—it is simply the inner silence. But if we use the words *inner silence*, you will not get the idea that there is some inspiration or some direction which is being pointed to. Hence the words *inner voice* have been used. But these are not the right words.

❋

We unnecessarily go on seeking advice from the outside when existence is ready to speak to us from the innermost core of our being. It is already there but we never listen to that still, small voice.

In fact, we cannot listen because we are living in such a noisy head, there is so much chattering going on. That still, small voice cannot penetrate unless you make your mind absolutely silent.

In many universities in America they have made a few experiments with total silence. Of course their experiments are concerned with the outer noise. It happened to a musician that he went into a chamber that was absolutely soundproof, no noise penetrated from the outside. He entered the chamber and he was surprised, because he was told there was absolute silence—and he was a trained musician, he was not deaf; he had an ear for sound. . . . He was very much puzzled; he started hearing two sounds. He rushed out and told the director, "What is the matter? I hear two sounds."

The director laughed; he said, "Yes, those two sounds will be there. One is of your heart beating and the other is of the blood circulating. Those we cannot stop because they go with you." The musician said, "I have never heard them before!"

Nobody ever hears them. But if you go into an absolutely silent chamber, one hundred percent soundproof, you will suddenly hear your heart beating—you cannot imagine that the heart beats so loudly, it is almost as if the sound is coming from the outside—and your blood circulating. Blood circulates with very great speed, it is a constant flow. It is riverlike; it has its own sound.

The same happens when your inner mind is completely silenced by meditative awareness. Then you hear the innermost advice . . . and you will be able to hear it in every situation. That is the finding of the inner guide.

The whole purpose of meditation is just to find the inner guide. Once you have found the inner guide, meditation also is no longer needed; then nothing is needed. You have got your eyes open, now you can live your life with total spontaneity. You need not depend on the memory system at all; now your answers will be real responses. Your actions will be real responses, not reactions.

Reactions come from the mind, responses come from the innermost core—and there is a vast difference, an immense distance between the two. A reaction is borrowed, hence you are not your own self. A *response* is yours; hence it fulfills you, it helps you to go on growing, to go on moving higher and higher. Finally, following the inner advice one comes to the point where one becomes absolutely harmonious with the whole, because when you go right always you become harmonious with the whole. That's exactly the meaning of right and wrong. Wrong means going astray from the whole, becoming discordant with the whole, and right means falling into harmony with the whole. And the whole has a direct connection with your being. You have to discover it, then it will become a truth to you.

III. Creativity

Creativity happens only when ego is absent, when you are relaxed, in deep rest, when there is really no desire to do something. Suddenly you are gripped; some unknown force overwhelms you, takes possession of you.

The only way to be really in tune with existence is to be creative. While you are creating something, whatsoever it is—poetry, a song, some music, some dance, whatsoever it is—whenever you are creating, you participate in existence. You are no longer separate from it; in fact, you disappear and existence starts creating through you. And if you can catch hold of those moments, if you become aware of those rare moments when there is no ego and creation is simply flowing through you, then creativity becomes meditative.

Every creator knows those moments, but in a vague way. Poets know that there are moments when poetry simply flows; even if you want to stop it you cannot stop it. And there are moments when you are simply dry, there are dry spells when you want to create something but nothing comes. The more effort you make, the less is the possibility . . . because the effort simply means ego effort.

Creativity happens only when ego is absent, when you are relaxed, in deep rest, when there is really no desire to do something. Suddenly you are gripped; some unknown force overwhelms you, takes possession of you. That is exactly the right word—you are possessed.

The poets, the painters, the sculptors, all know these moments but they know them only when they are gone. They only remember them; they look back and they feel that something of great importance was there, but it is no more. They catch hold of those moments only when they are gone. The meditator catches hold of them while they are there. That's the only difference between the poet and the mystic: the poet remembers the creative moments, the mystic becomes aware in those moments themselves. And that makes a great difference.

Once you have become aware that you are not and still you are—that the ego is no longer there, the self is no longer there, still you are—you have had a totally new experience of your own being. Buddha calls it nirvana, no-selfness. And the creator comes to it many times; the only thing is that he should catch hold of it while it is there.

Meditation is just to catch hold of those moments—and creativity is to create those moments. When creativity and meditation meet, you have arrived home; the journey is complete.

IV. The Rebel

The situation of the rebel is tremendously exciting: each moment he is faced with problems because the society has a fixed mode, a fixed pattern, fixed ideals. And the rebel cannot go with those fixed ideals—he has to follow his own still, small voice.

The rebel is renouncing the past. He is not going to repeat the past; he is bringing something new into the world. Those who have escaped from the world and society are escapists. They have really renounced responsibilities, but without understanding that the moment you renounce responsibilities you also renounce freedom. These are the complexities of life: freedom and responsibilities go away together or remain together.

The more you are a lover of freedom, the more you will be ready to accept responsibilities. But outside the world, outside the society, there is no possibility of any responsibility. And it has to be remembered that all we learn, we learn through being responsible.

The past has destroyed the beauty of the word *responsibility*. People have made it almost equivalent to duty; it is not really so. A duty is something done reluctantly, as part of your spiritual slavery. Duty to your elders, duty to your husband, duty to your children—they are not responsibilities.

To understand the word *responsibility* is very significant. You have to break it in two: response and ability. You can act in two ways—one is reaction, another is response. Reaction comes out of your past conditionings; it is mechanical. Response comes out of your presence, awareness, consciousness; it is non-mechanical. And the ability to respond is one of the greatest principles of growth. You are not following any order, any commandment; you are simply following your awareness. You are functioning like a mirror, reflecting the situation and responding to it—not out of your memory, from past experiences of similar situations, not repeating your reactions, but acting fresh, new, in this very moment. Neither is the situation old, nor is your response—both are new. This ability is one of the qualities of the rebel.

V. No-Thingness

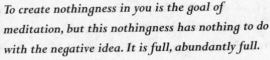

To create nothingness in you is the goal of meditation, but this nothingness has nothing to do with the negative idea. It is full, abundantly full.

It is so full that it starts overflowing. Buddha has defined this nothingness as overflowing compassion.

Nothingness can either be just emptiness or it can be a tremendous fullness. It can be negative, it can be positive. If it is negative it is like death, darkness. Religions have called it hell. It is hell because there is no joy in it, no song in it; there is no heartbeat, no dance. Nothing flowers, nothing opens. One is simply empty.

This empty nothingness has created great fear in people. That's why, in the West particularly, God has never been called nothingness except by a few mystics like Dionysius, Eckhart, Boehme; but they are not the main current of Western thinking. The West has always conceived nothingness in negative terms; hence it has created a tremendous fear about it. And they go on saying to people that the empty mind is the devil's workshop.

The East has known its positive aspect too; it is one of the greatest contributions to human consciousness. Buddha will laugh at this statement that emptiness is the devil's workshop. He will say: Only in emptiness, only in nothingness, does godliness happen. But he is talking about the positive phenomenon.

For Gautam Buddha, for Mahavira, for the long tradition of Zen Masters and the Taoists, nothingness simply means no-thingness. All *things* have disappeared, and because things have disappeared there is pure consciousness left behind. The mirror is empty of any reflection, but the mirror is there. Consciousness is empty of content, but consciousness is there. When it was full of content, so many things were inside that you could not have known what consciousness is. When the consciousness is full of contents, that's what we call mind. When consciousness is empty of all contents, that's what we call no-mind or meditation.

To create nothingness in you is the goal of meditation, but this nothingness has nothing to do with the negative idea. It is full, abundantly full. It is so full that it starts overflowing. Buddha has defined this nothingness as overflowing compassion.

The word *compassion* is beautiful. It is made out of the same word as "passion." When passion is transformed, when the desire to seek and search for the other is no longer there—when you are enough unto yourself, when you don't need anybody, when the very desire for the other has evaporated—when you are utterly happy, blissful, just being alone, then passion becomes compassion.

Only nothingness can be infinite; somethingness is bound to be finite. Only out of nothingness is an infinite expanse of life, existence, possible—not out of somethingness. God is not "somebody." He is nobody or, more correctly, nobodiness. God is not "something." He is nothing or, even more correctly, no-thingness. He is a creative void— what Buddha has called *shunya*. He is a creative void.

Remember, nothingness does not mean that it is nothing; nothingness simply means that it is all. Nothingness means "no-thingness." Things are forms; nothingness is a formless energy. It can manifest in millions of forms, and it can only manifest in millions of forms because it has no form of its own. It is fluid, it is available for any form, it has no resistance to any form. It can express itself in millions of ways because it has no obsession, it has no fixation. It can bloom as a rose, it can bloom as a lotus. It can be a song, it can be a dance, it can be silence. All is possible because nothingness simply means that no form has yet been taken. Once a form is taken, things become limited, alternatives become limited. Once a form is taken you are not totally free; your form becomes your bondage. Hence, meditation is an entry into nothingness.

Thought is a world; hence Buddha calls mind "the world." The moment a thought arises, a wave has arisen in the lake of consciousness, a form has arisen, and the form is only temporal, momentary. Soon it will disappear; it is not going to abide, it is not eternal. Don't cling to it. Watch it come in and watch it go out. Watch it arising and watch it disappearing, but don't cling to it. Remember consciousness, in which it arises and in which it dissolves again. That is your reality, that is your truth.

VI. The Lovers

To others it will look like madness—in fact all love is mad and all love is blind, at least to those who don't know what love is. To "unlovers" love is blind; to lovers, love is the only possible eye that can see to the very core of existence.

Love is the goal—life is the journey. And a journey without a goal is bound to be neurotic, haphazard; it will not have any direction. One day you are going north and another day you are going south. It will remain accidental—anything can lead you anywhere. You will remain like driftwood unless the goal is clear.

The word *intimacy* comes from a Latin root, *intimum*. *Intimum* means your interiority, your innermost core. Unless you have something there, you can't be intimate with anybody. You cannot allow *intimum*, intimacy, because the other person will see the hole, the wound, and the pus oozing out of it. He will see that you don't know who you are, that you are a madman, that you don't know where you are going, that you have not even heard your own song, that your life is a chaos, it is not a cosmos. Hence the fear of intimacy. Even lovers rarely become intimate. And just to be sexually related to somebody is not intimacy. The genital orgasm is not all that is there in intimacy. It is just the periphery of it; intimacy can exist with it, can exist without it.

Intimacy is a totally different dimension. It is allowing the other to come into you, to see you as you see yourself, to allow the other to see you from your inside, to invite somebody to that deepest core of your being. In the modern world intimacy is disappearing. Even lovers are not intimate. Friendship is only a word now—it has disappeared. And the reason? The reason is that there is nothing to share. Who wants to show one's inner poverty? One wants to pretend: "I am rich, I have arrived, I know what I am doing, I know where I am going."

One is not ready and courageous enough to open up, to show one's inner chaos and to be vulnerable. The other may exploit it—that fear is there. The other may become too dominant. Seeing that you are a chaos, seeing that you need a master, that you are not a master of your own being, the other may become the master. Hence everybody tries to protect themselves so nobody knows their inner helplessness; otherwise they can be exploited. This world consists of much exploitation.

Love is the goal, and once the goal is clear you start growing an inner richness. The wound disappears and becomes a lotus; the wound is transformed into a lotus. That is the miracle of love, the magic of love. Love is the greatest alchemical force in the world. Those who know how to use it can reach the highest peak.

When you don't need a person at all, when you are totally sufficient unto yourself, when you can be alone and tremendously happy and ecstatic, then love is possible. But then too you cannot be certain whether the other's love is real or not—you can be certain about only one thing: whether *your* love is real. How can you be certain about the other? But then there is no need.

But while you are asleep you will need somebody's love—even if it is false, you will need it. Enjoy it! Don't create anxiety. And try to become more and more awake.

One day when you are really awake you will be able to love—but then you will be certain only about your love. But that's enough! Who bothers? Right now, you want to use others. When you are really blissful on your own, you don't want to use anybody. You simply want to share. You have so much, so much is overflowing, you would like somebody to share it. And you will feel thankful that somebody was ready to receive.

Right now, you are worried too much whether the other really loves you—because you are not certain about your own love. You are not certain about your worth. You cannot believe that somebody can really love you. You don't see anything in yourself. You cannot love yourself—how can somebody else love you? It seems unreal, it seems impossible.

Do you love yourself? You have not even asked the question. People hate themselves. People condemn themselves—they go on condemning; they go on thinking that they are rotten. How can the other love you? Such a rotten person. No, nobody can love you really. The other must be fooling, cheating; there must be some other reason. She must be after something else; he must be after something else.

There is no way to be certain about the other—first be certain about yourself. And a person who is certain about himself is certain about the whole world.

VII. Awareness

You are awareness. It is nothing you do, it is nothing that has to be done—your very nature is awareness.

Awareness is not part of the mind. It flows through the mind, but it is not part of the mind. It is just like a lightbulb—the electricity flows through it, but the electricity is not part of the bulb. If you break the bulb, you have not broken electricity. The expression will be hindered, but the potentiality remains hidden. You put another bulb in and the electricity starts flowing.

Mind is just an instrument. Awareness is not part of it, but awareness flows through it. When mind is transcended, awareness remains in itself. That's why I say even a buddha will have to use the mind if he talks to you, if he relates to you, because then he will need the flow, the flow of his inner pool. He will have to use instruments, mediums, and then the mind will function. But the mind is just a vehicle.

Mind is just the vehicle. And you are not using the mind to its total capacity. If you use it to its total capacity, it will become what Buddha calls "right knowledge." We are using our minds like someone who uses an airplane like a bus. You can cut the wings of the airplane and use it like a bus on the road. That will do; it will work like a bus. But you are foolish. That bus can fly! You are not using it to its right capacity.

You are using your mind for dreams, imaginations, madness. You have not used it, you have cut the wings. If you use it with wings, it can become right knowledge; it can become wisdom. But that too is part of the mind; that too is the vehicle. The user remains behind; the user cannot be the used. *You* are using it, *you* are awareness. And all efforts for meditation are to know this awareness in its purity, without any medium.

And this can be known only when mind has stopped functioning. When mind has stopped functioning, you will become aware that awareness is there; you are filled with it. Mind was just a vehicle, a passage. Now, if you want, you can use the mind, and if you don't want, you need not use it.

Body and mind, both are vehicles. You are not the vehicle, you are the master hidden behind these vehicles. But you have forgotten completely and you have become the cart; you have become the vehicle. This is what Gurdjieff calls identification. This is what, in India, yogis have called *tadatmya*, becoming one with something that you are not.

When we say the mind ceases, we mean your identification is broken. Now you know that *this* is the mind and *this* is "I am." The bridge is broken. Now the mind is not the master. It has become just an instrument; it has fallen to its right place. So whenever you need it, you can use it.

Just by witnessing, mind doesn't cease and the brain cells will not cease. Rather, they will become more alive because there will be less conflict, more energy. They will become fresher. And you can use them more rightly, more accurately, but you will not be burdened by them and they will not force you to do something. They will not push and pull you here and there. You will be the master.

How does it happen just by witnessing? Because the bondage has happened by *not* witnessing. The bondage has happened because you are not alert, so the bondage will disappear if you become alert. The bondage is only unawareness. Nothing else is needed: become more alert, whatsoever you do.

Whatsoever you do, make it a point not to do it in a sleepy way. Watch every act, every thought, every feeling. Watch and move. Every moment is very precious—don't waste it in sleepiness. And if you use every moment as an opportunity to become more conscious, the consciousness grows by and by. One day, suddenly, you find that the light is burning inside. If you work hard towards it, one day suddenly in the morning you rise completely new—dry, unattached; loving, but not in any way involved; remaining in the world and yet a watcher on the hills. This is the paradox that has to be fulfilled: remaining in the world and yet watching from the hills; at the same time, simultaneously, being in the world and not being in it.

That is how base metals are transformed into gold. With unconsciousness you are a base metal, with consciousness you will become gold, you are transformed. Just the fire of awareness is needed. You lack nothing else, everything is there. With the fire of awareness a new arrangement happens.

VIII. Courage

Growth certainly needs one thing, and that is courage. That is the most fundamental religious quality. Everything else is ordinary and can follow, but courage is the most fundamental thing, the first thing.

You are a seed. The seed can have four possibilities.

The seed may remain a seed forever, closed, windowless, not in communion with existence, dead, because life means communion with existence. And the seed *is* dead, it has not yet communicated with the earth, with the sky, with the air, with the wind, with the sun, with the stars. It has not yet made any attempt to have a dialogue with all that exists. It is utterly lonely, enclosed, encapsulated into itself, surrounded by a Great Wall of China. The seed lives in its own grave.

The first possibility is that the seed may remain a seed. That is very unfortunate—a man may remain simply a seed. With all the potential at your disposal, with all the blessings ready to shower on you, you may never open your doors.

The second possibility is that the seed may be courageous enough, may dive deep into the soil, may die as an ego, may drop its armor, may start a communion with existence, may become one with the earth. Great courage is needed, because who knows? This death may be ultimate, there may be no birth following it. What is the guarantee? There is no guarantee; it is a gamble. Only a few gather courage enough to gamble, to risk.

To be a seeker is the beginning of the gamble. You are risking your life, you are risking your ego. You are risking because you are dropping all your securities, all your safety arrangements. You are opening windows—who knows who is going to come in? The friend or the enemy—who knows? You are becoming vulnerable. That's what seeking is all about. That's what Buddha was teaching his whole life. Forty-two years continuously, transforming seeds into plants—that was his work—transforming ordinary human beings into seekers.

A seeker is a plant, a sprout—soft, delicate. The seed is never in danger, remember. What danger can there be for the seed? It is absolutely protected. But the plant is always in danger, the plant is very soft. The seed is like a stone, hard, hidden behind a hard crust. But the plant has to pass through a thousand and one hazards. That is the second stage: the seed dissolving into the soil, the man disappearing as an ego, disappearing as a personality, becoming a plant.

The third possibility, which is even more rare, because not all plants are going to attain that height where they can bloom into flowers, a thousand and one flowers. . . . Very few human beings attain the second stage, and very few of those who attain the second stage attain the third, the stage of the flower. Why can't they attain the third stage, the stage of the flower? Because of greed, because of miserliness, they are not ready to share . . . because of a state of unlovingness.

Courage is needed to become a plant, and love is needed to become a flower. A flower means the tree is opening up its heart, releasing its perfume, giving its soul, pouring its being into existence. The seed can become a plant, although it is difficult to drop the armor, but in one way it is simple. The seed will only be gathering more and more, accumulating more and more; the seed only takes from the soil. The tree only takes from the water, from the air, from the sun; its greed is not disturbed; on the contrary, its ambition is fulfilled. It goes on becoming bigger and bigger. But a moment comes when you have taken so much that now you have to share. You have been benefited so much, now you have to serve. God has given you so much, now you have to thank, be grateful—and the only way to be grateful is to shower your treasures, give them back to existence, be as unmiserly as existence has been with you. Then the tree grows into flowers, it blossoms.

And the fourth stage is that of fragrance. The flower is still gross, it is still material, but the fragrance is subtle, it is almost something non-material. You cannot see it, it is invisible. You can only smell it, you cannot grab it, you cannot grasp it. A very sensitive understanding is needed to have a dialogue with the fragrance. And beyond fragrance there is nothing. The fragrance disappears into the universe, becomes one with it.

These are the four stages of the seed, and these are the four stages of human beings too. Don't remain a seed. Gather courage—courage to drop the ego, courage to drop the securities, courage to drop the safeties, courage to be vulnerable. But then don't remain a tree, because a tree without flowers is poor. A tree without flowers is empty, a tree without flowers is missing something essential. It has no beauty—without love there is no beauty. And it is only through flowers that the tree shows its love. It has taken so much from the sun and the moon and from the earth; now it is time to give.

IX. Aloneness

There are a few things that can only be done alone. Love, prayer, life, death, aesthetic experiences, blissful moments—they all come when you are alone

Nobody wants to be alone. The greatest fear in the world is to be left alone. People do a thousand and one things just not to be left alone. You imitate your neighbors so you are just like them and you are not left alone. You lose your individuality, you lose your uniqueness. You just become imitators, because if you are not imitators you will be left alone.

You become part of the crowd, you become part of a church, you become part of an organization. Somehow you want to merge with a crowd where you can feel at ease, that you are not alone, there are so many people like you—so many Mohammedans like you, so many Hindus like you, so many Christians, millions of them . . . you are not alone.

To be alone is really the greatest miracle. That means now you don't belong to any church, you don't belong to any organization, you don't belong to any theology, you don't belong to any ideology—socialist, communist, fascist, Hindu, Christian, Jain, Buddhist—you don't belong, you simply are. And you have learned how to love your indefinable, ineffable reality. You have come to know how to be with yourself.

Try to understand this. You are born alone; you die alone. These two are the greatest moments in life: birth and death. You are born alone; you die alone. The greatest moments of life—the beginning and the end—are in aloneness. When you meditate, you again become alone. That's why meditation is both—a death and a birth. You die to the past and you are born to the new, to the unknown.

Even in love, when you think you are together, you are not

together. There are two alonenesses. In real love nothing is lost. When two lovers are sitting—if they are really lovers and they don't try to possess each other and they don't try to dominate each other, because that is not love; that is the way of hatred, the way of violence—if they love, and if the love is coming out of their aloneness, you will see two beautiful alonenesses together. They are like two Himalayan peaks, high in the sky, but separate. They don't interfere. In fact, deep love only reveals your pure aloneness to you.

All that is true and all that is real will always bring you to aloneness. Love, prayer, life, death, aesthetic experiences, blissful moments—they all come when you are alone. When you are in love you think you are with somebody. Maybe the somebody is just reflecting your aloneness, the somebody is just a mirror in which your aloneness is reflected. But the deeper you move in love, the deeper you know that even your lover cannot penetrate there. Your aloneness is absolute—and it is good that it is so; otherwise you will be a public thing. Then you will not have any innermost core where you can be alone. Then you can be violated. But your aloneness is absolute; nobody can violate it.

X. Change

Only the entry of the new can transform you, there is no other way of transformation.

If you allow the new to enter, you will never be the same again.

The new does not arise out of you, it comes from the beyond. It is not part of you. The new is discontinuous with you, hence the fear. Your whole past is at stake. You have lived in one way, you have thought in one way, you have made a comfortable life out of your beliefs. Then something new knocks on the door. Now your whole past pattern is going to be disturbed. If you allow the new to enter, you will never be the same again, the new will transform you.

It is risky. With the new, one never knows where one will end. The old is known, familiar; you have lived with it for long, you are acquainted with it. The new is unfamiliar. It may be a friend, it may be an enemy, who knows. And there is no way to know. The only way to know is to allow it; hence the apprehension, the fear.

And you cannot keep rejecting it either, because the old has not yet given you what you seek. The old has been promising, but the promises have not been fulfilled. The old is familiar but miserable. The new is maybe going to be uncomfortable . . . but there is a possibility—it may bring bliss to you. So you cannot reject it and you cannot accept it either; hence you waver, you tremble, great anguish arises in your being. It is natural, this is how it has always been. This is how it will always be.

Try to understand the appearance of the new. Everybody in the world wants to become new, because nobody is satisfied with the old. Nobody can ever be satisfied with the old because whatever it is, you have known it. Once known it has become repetitive; once known it has become boring, monotonous. You want to get rid of it. You want to explore, you want to adventure. You want to become new . . . and yet when the new knocks on the door you shrink back, you withdraw, you hide in the old. This is the dilemma.

How do we become new?—and everybody wants to become new. Courage is needed, and not ordinary courage; extraordinary courage is needed. And the world is full of cowards, hence people have stopped growing. How can you grow if you are a coward? With each new opportunity you shrink back, you close your eyes. How can you grow? How can you be? You only pretend to be.

How do we become new? We do not become new of ourselves. Newness comes from the beyond. Newness comes from existence. Mind is always old. Mind is never new, it is the accumulation of the past. Newness comes from the beyond; it is a gift. It is from the beyond and it is of the beyond.

The unknown and the unknowable, the beyond, has ingress into you. It has ingress into you because you are never sealed and set apart; you are not an island. You may have forgotten the beyond but the beyond has not forgotten you. The child may have forgotten the mother, the mother has not forgotten the child. The part may have started thinking, "I am separate," but the whole knows that you are not separate. The whole has ingress in you. It is still in contact with you. That's why the new goes on coming although you don't welcome it. It comes every morning, it comes every evening. It comes in a thousand and one ways. If you have eyes to see, you will see it continuously coming to you.

And only the new, accepted deeply and totally, can transform you. You cannot bring the new in your life; the new comes. You can either accept it or reject it. If you reject it you remain a stone, closed and dead. If you receive it you become a flower, you start opening . . . and in that opening is celebration.

The new is a messenger, the new is a message. It is a gospel. Listen to the new, go with the new. I know you are afraid. In spite of the fear, go with the new, and your life will become richer and richer and you will be able one day to release the imprisoned splendor.

The moment anything becomes a repetition you start behaving like a robot. And everything is bound to become a repetition, unless your intelligence, your meditativeness, your love is so great that it goes on transforming you, and the person you love. So that each time you look in the eyes of the person you love, it is something different, it is something new—new flowers have blossomed, the season has changed.

Unless one remains changing, even love becomes hell; otherwise, everybody would be in love in the whole world, but everybody is living in his own hell—private hells, just like attached bathrooms. To live a life that never becomes a misery, that never becomes a hell, one has to be fresh every moment, unburdened of the past, always trying to find new dimensions to relate with people, new ways to relate with people, new songs to sing. One should make it a point, a basic point, that "I will not live like a machine." The machine has no life—it has efficiency. The world needs you to be a machine because the world needs efficiency. But your own being needs you to be absolutely non-mechanical, unpredictable—each morning should find you new.

XI. Breakthrough

In English we have two words, very beautiful, of great significance: one is **breakdown,** *the other is* **breakthrough.** *Breakdown is when you don't know any meditation and your logic becomes irrelevant. Then there is a breakthrough: you enter into a new world, a new vision, a new perspective.*

If your head comes to a breakdown, don't be worried. Use the opportunity of this de-structured state. In that moment, don't be worried that you are going mad; in that moment, slip into the heart.

Someday, in the future, when psychology really comes of age, whenever somebody goes mad from the head we will help him to move towards the heart—because an opportunity opens in that moment. The breakdown can become a breakthrough. The old structure is gone, now he is no longer in the clutches of reason. He is free for a moment. Modern psychology tries to go on adjusting the person back to the old structure. All modern efforts are adjustive: how to make the person normal again. The real psychology will do something else. The real psychology will use this opportunity . . . because the old mind has disappeared, there is a gap. Use this interval and lead the person toward another mind—that is, the heart. Lead him toward another center of being.

When you drive a car you change gears. Whenever you change the gear, there comes a moment when the gear moves through neutral; it has to move through the neutral gear. Neutral gear means no gear. From one gear to another, a moment comes when there is no gear. When one mind has failed, you are in a neutral state. Just now you are again as if you are just born. Use this opportunity and lead the energy away from the old rotten structure, which is falling. Leave the ruin. Move into the heart. Forget reason and let love be your center, your target. Each breakdown can become a breakthrough, and each possibility for the failure of the head can become a success for the heart—the failure of the head can become a success for the heart.

There are layers of energy. The first layer is a very tiny layer. It is only for day-to-day use—getting up in the morning, taking your breakfast, taking a bath, going to the office, earning your bread, coming back; that kind of work. That is a very small layer.

When you start meditating, energy is being taken from the first layer, and that is a new kind of work. The old work continues and new energy is not yet available. If you go on celebrating there comes a point when you feel really, utterly exhausted. Only then, in that utter exhaustion, will there be a breakthrough and from the second layer energy will start flowing in you. Then you will never be tired. On the contrary, you will feel you have more energy than you can use; you have stumbled upon a deeper source of energy. That is the second source—it is enormous.

It happens in situations, in ordinary situations too: you are tired—you have come from the office, utterly tired—you want to go to sleep. Suddenly your house is on fire and all tiredness disappears. The second layer is the emergency layer. When there is really a situation where it is a question of life and death, then it becomes available. You are full of energy—no sleep, nothing, no tiredness. You will come to that layer slowly, slowly.

Then there is a third layer, which is not human at all. The first is individual, the second is collective, the third is cosmic. Very few people reach the third. To reach the third is to become enlightened.

XII. New Vision

Spirituality is not the practicing of any virtue; spirituality is the gaining of a new vision. Virtue follows that vision; it comes on its own accord. It is a natural by-product.

When you start seeing, things start changing.

This is a beginning, the beginning of a new life, the beginning of a new vision . . . the beginning of a new way of being. You will have to drop much, you will have to disconnect yourself from all that is gone, from the past. Don't carry it anymore. It is an unnecessary burden. It hinders growth, it paralyzes. Slowly, slowly it becomes such a mountain that one is crushed underneath the mountain.

One should be capable of dying to the past every moment so that it is never accumulated.

That's the path of the seeker—dying to the past every moment so that you are always young and fresh and alive, so that you are always present in the present.

To be present in the present is to be present before God.

When you start dropping your ego, which is the cause of your death, you start attaining to a new vision of life, a new style of life. You are resurrected. But it needs a humble heart, one who is not egoistic, one who is ready to surrender, one who can say to God, "Let thy will be done."

God is not a person whom you are going to meet some day. God is an experience—the experience of your dissolution, of your ego disappearing. And when your ego is no more, what is left? Just a pure vastness, an infinite nothingness exists. But that nothingness is not negative; that nothingness is a new kind of fullness. It is nothingness from the side of the ego, it is fullness from the side of the whole. It is nothingness from the old vision—but it is a new birth, and a new vision is born.

And it is overflowing. It is overflowing with power. And this power is eternal; this power has no beginning, no end.

Mind is confusion. Thoughts and thoughts—thousands of thoughts clamoring, clashing, fighting with each other, fighting for your attention. Thousands of thoughts are pulling you into thousands of directions. It is a miracle how you go on keeping yourself together. Somehow you manage this togetherness—it is only somehow, it is only a facade. Deep behind it there is a clamoring crowd, a civil war, a continuous civil war. Thoughts fighting with each other, thoughts wanting you to fulfill them—it is a great confusion, what you call your mind.

But if you are aware that the mind is confusion, and you don't get identified with the mind, you will never fall. You will become fallproof! The mind will become impotent. And because you will be watching continuously, your energies will slowly be withdrawn, away from the mind; it will not be nourished anymore.

And once the mind dies, you are born as a no-mind. That birth is enlightenment. That birth brings you for the first time to the land of peace, the lotus paradise. It brings you to the world of bliss, benediction. Otherwise you remain in hell. Right now you are in hell. But if you resolve, if you decide, if you choose consciousness, right now you can take a jump, a leap from hell into heaven.

XIII. Transformation

The art of transforming suffering, pain, evil, into something good is the art of seeing the necessity of the opposite.

Only through that acceptance is transformation possible.

The art of transforming suffering, pain, evil, into something good is the art of seeing the necessity of the opposite. Light can exist only if darkness exists. Then why hate darkness? Without darkness there will be no light, so those who love light and hate darkness are in a dilemma; they don't know what they are doing.

Life cannot exist without death. Then why hate death? Because it is death that creates the space for life to exist. This is a great insight, that death is the contrast, the background, the blackboard on which life is written with white chalk. Death is the darkness of night on which life starts twinkling like stars. If you destroy the darkness of the night the stars will disappear. That's what happens in the day. The stars are still there—do you think they have disappeared? They are still there, but because there is too much light, you cannot see them. They can be seen only in contrast.

The saint is possible only because of the sinner. Hence, Buddha says don't hate the sinner. He makes it possible for the saint to exist; they are two aspects of the same coin. Seeing this, one is neither attached to good nor detached from bad. One accepts both as part and parcel of life. In that acceptance you can transform things. Only through that acceptance is transformation possible.

And before you can transform suffering you will have to become a witness; that is the third point. First: do not resist evil. Second: know that opposites are not opposites but complementaries, inevitably joined together, so there is no choice—remain choiceless. And the third is: be a witness, because if you are a witness to your suffering you will be able to absorb it. If you become identified with it you cannot absorb it.

The moment you become identified with your suffering you want to discard it, you want to get rid of it, it is so painful. But if you are a witness then suffering loses all thorns, all stings. Then there is suffering, and you are a witness to it. You are just a mirror; it has nothing to do with you. Happiness comes and goes, unhappiness comes and goes, it is a passing show; you are just there, a mirror reflecting it. Life comes and goes, death comes and goes; the mirror is not affected by either. The mirror reflects but remains unaffected; the mirror is not imprinted by either.

A great distance arises when you witness. And only in that witnessing can you become able to transform the base metal into gold. Only in that witnessing do you become a scientist of the inner, a detached observer. Now you know the opposites are not opposites, so they can be changed into each other. Then it is not a question of destroying evil in the world, but of transforming evil into something beneficial; transforming poison into nectar.

It is always worth considering, "Am I blissful the way I am living?" If one is not then one must take risks. New paths, new life styles, a new search will have to be undertaken. This much is certain: you have nothing to lose. You did not find bliss through your old life style. If you had there would be no need for the new. The old has become meaningless, this much is certain. The new can turn out to be meaningful or it can turn out to be meaningless. But at least in the new there is a possibility of it being meaningful. The old has been through the press. You have seen it, understood it, and lived it without receiving anything. As if one had been trying to extract oil from sand. How long will you wrack your brains trying to get oil from sand?

I do not say that the new will definitely give you bliss, because bliss is less dependent on the path than on the traveler, the one who travels on it. Hence the real change is not in the path, the real change is in the traveler. But to change paths is a beginning.

You are outside, so the transformation also has to begin from the outside. If you gather courage to change the outside it will strengthen your courage to change inside. And if a few drops of bliss start showering on you then the search for the new will begin with joy and eagerness.

XIV. Integration

At your very center you are integrated, otherwise you could not exist at all. How can you exist without a center?

Integration has nothing to do with "becoming." In fact, all efforts to "become" bring disintegration.

Integration is already there at the deepest core of your being; it has not to be brought in. At your very center you are integrated, otherwise you could not exist at all. How can you exist without a center? The bullock-cart moves, the wheel moves, because there is an unmoving center on which the wheel moves. It moves on the hub. If the cart is moving the hub is there. You may know it, you may not know it.

You are alive, you are breathing, you are conscious; life is moving, so there must be a hub to the wheel of life. You may not be aware, but it is there. Without it, you cannot be.

So the first thing, and very fundamental: becoming is not the issue. You are. You have just to go in and see it. It is a discovery, not an achievement. You have been carrying it all along. But you have become too attached to the periphery, and your back is to the center. You have become too outgoing, so you cannot look in.

Create a little insight. The word *insight* is beautiful—it means to have sight in, to look in, to see in. Eyes open outward, hands spread outward, legs move away from you. Sit silently, relax the periphery, close your eyes, and just go in . . . and not with effort. Just relax—as if one is drowning and one cannot do anything. We go on "doing" even when we are drowning.

If you can simply allow it to happen, it will surface. Out of the clouds you will see the center arising.

There is one of the most ancient meditations still used in some monasteries of Tibet. The meditation is based on the truth that I am saying to you. They teach that sometimes you can simply disappear. Sitting in the garden, you just start feeling that you are disappearing. Just see how the world looks when you have gone from the world, when you are no longer here, when you have become absolutely transparent. Just try for a single second not to be. In your own home, be as if you are not.

It is really a beautiful meditation. You can try it many times in twenty-four hours. Just half a second will do; for half a second, simply stop . . . you are not . . . and the world continues. When you become more and more alert to the fact that without you the world continues perfectly well, then you will be able to learn another part of your being which has been neglected for long, for lives—and that is the receptive mode. You simply allow, you become a door. Things go on happening without you.

First attain to the receptive mode, first attain to the passive, first attain to the non-active. And when your inner being flowers and you have come to know the integration inside—which is always there, the center is always there.

You are already integrated. Not on the periphery—on the periphery there is much turmoil. You are fragmented on the periphery. Move inward, and the deeper you go, the more you will find that you are integrated. There comes a point, at the very innermost shrine of your being, where you suddenly find you are a unity, an absolute unity.

XV. Conditioning

Whatever you have learned from others is not you. That is your persona, and you have to find your innocence again. You have to find your essence before people started putting layers on you, before people started civilizing you.

An ancient parable in the East is that a lioness, while taking a jump from one hillock to another hillock, in the middle of the jump gave birth to a child. The cub fell, on the way, into a crowd of sheep. The sheep nourished the cub, not knowing that it was a lion—their enemy. And the cub never came to know that he was a lion because everybody around him was a sheep. So he walked in the crowd of sheep, just like a sheep.

Sheep never walk alone; they walk as a crowd, almost stepping on each other, rubbing their bodies against each other. They are afraid to be alone; it is dangerous to be alone, any wild animal can catch hold of them—they have to be together.

Lions walk alone, never in a crowd.

Lions have a very big territory. They don't want anybody to enter their territory. Sometimes one lion will have an area of miles as his territory. No other lion can even manage to get in; otherwise there is going to be a ferocious fight till one is dead, or perhaps both are dead. And they walk alone.

But this poor lion had no idea that he was a lion; he had no idea how he looked. He became bigger and bigger, but the sheep had become accustomed to him; they had been bringing him up from his very childhood. Although he was a strange sheep, he was a sheep . . . because he used to eat grass, which lions don't eat. They would rather die than eat grass. He used to eat grass—he remained vegetarian. He used to go into the crowd, just in the middle, to be safe, although he was taller, bigger . . . but without any idea of it. And he never roared once like a lion, because if you don't have that idea, how can you roar? He dreamed like a sheep, feared like a sheep, was afraid of wild animals that could not do any harm to him.

One day an old lion saw this scene. He could not believe his eyes! The young lion was so big, and he had never seen a lion and sheep mixing. There has never been any friendship, there is no possibility. But the sheep were moving with the lion without any fear, and the lion was also moving with the sheep, afraid to be alone.

The old lion could not believe his eyes. He ran after the crowd. Naturally, all the sheep started running and making the noise sheep make. And the young lion was also making the same noise. It took much effort—only with great difficulty could the old lion catch hold of the young lion. And the young lion was crying and weeping, just like a sheep.

The old lion dragged the young fellow to a nearby pond. The young lion was very much afraid; he was not willing to go, he was very reluctant. And he was more powerful than the old lion. If the young lion had known that he was a lion, the old lion would not have been able to pull him to the pond; he would have killed him! But he was a sheep, so he allowed the old lion to pull him—although reluctantly, unwillingly, resisting, knowing that this was sure death, because many sheep had died, had been killed by the lions. Now his turn had come.

But at the pond a miracle happened: the old lion said to the young one, "My son, just look into the pond"—where they both were reflected. And there was a sudden transformation, because the sheep was not a reality, it was just a false idea implanted by the society in which the lion was brought up. It was his personality, but not his individuality. It was his ego, but not his real self. It was just a mask, but not his original face.

For the first time he looked at both the faces; and suddenly there was a roar. From the depths of his being came a great roar shaking the hills around.

The old lion said, "My work is done. All that I could do, I have done—now you are on your own. Now you know who you are."

Personality is that which is given to you by the society, culture, civilization, education; in other words, by others. People are giving you their opinion about you, and you are collecting those opinions. Those opinions are creating your personality.

You must have observed very small children whose personalities are not yet developed. It takes time. For at least three or four years the child remains more of an individual than he may ever be again. He is authentic, sincere. He does not take any note of others' opinions.

It is because of this that if you want to remember your past you can go back only up to a certain moment—and that moment will be the age of either four years or three years, at the most three years. After that there is a complete blank. You have been here during those three years, but you don't remember anything. You were nine months in your mother's womb—you don't remember anything at all.

The reason you cannot now remember these three years is because you had no personality. It is the personality which accumulates the opinions of others and creates a false identity, a certain idea of "Who I am." You don't know exactly who you are, because to know who you are, you will have to dig deep within yourself through all the rubbish that has accumulated in the name of personality. You will have to become a child again.

What you know about yourself is your personality. You know that you have a certain name—are you aware that you came into the world without a name? You have a certain education, a certain qualification—you know you were not born a doctor or an engineer or a professor. These are things added to you. Your degrees, your name, your fame . . . all these things are added to you. But this is what you are; as far as you are concerned, if all these things are taken away from you, what will you be? Just a zero . . . a plain slate, all writing has been removed.

Your personality is all that you know about yourself—I am making it absolutely simple so that you can be alert—and your individuality is that which you *don't* know, and you *are*.

Meditation is an effort to get rid of personality and to reach your living sources of life, your individuality, the flame that you have brought from your mother's womb—and that you had before your birth, even before you entered the womb of the mother. You have had your individuality since eternity. It is your essential consciousness, which is covered with so many layers of so many lives that it is lost completely and you have forgotten the way back to it.

So remember: whatever you have learned from others is not you. That is your persona, and you have to find your innocence again. You have to find your essence before people started putting layers on you, before people started civilizing you, making you more cultured, more educated.

XVI. Thunderbolt

*Man forgets many things intentionally. He tries
not to remember, because remembering may smash
all his ego and bring it all crashing down. But in
this life, we get as much as we are willing to give
up and let go.*

If a small glimpse of the truth comes to you, you
will be upset, you won't be able to understand.

Have you noticed? Sometimes something suddenly wakes you up
when you were deeply asleep. At five A.M. you were sound asleep, at
the hour of deepest sleep, and something suddenly awakens you. Some
noise, some firecracker goes off in the street, a car crashes into your
door, some noise that immediately wakes you up. Instantly—you
jump immediately from sleep to wakefulness. You come like an arrow
from the depths of sleep. Usually when we come out of deep sleep we
come very slowly. First deep sleep drops away, then dreams gradually
start floating, then we remain in dreams for a while. But if something
happens suddenly, you come like an arrow from the depths straight to
awakening. Your eyes open and you wonder: Where am I? Who am I?
For a moment nothing is clear.

This must have happened to all of you at some time or other. You
wonder, "Who am I?" Even your name and address will be gone.
"Where am I?" This too will be unclear. It is as if you have suddenly
come to some alien world. It lasts only a moment, then you come back
together, because this shock isn't such a great shock. And then too you are
used to it—it happens every day. You get up every morning: you return
from the world of dreams into the world of wakefulness. This routine
is old, yet sometimes when it happens suddenly, you are startled and
frightened.

When the real awakening happens you will be completely speechless. You won't have any idea what is happening. Everything will become calm and silent.

Keep what I am saying to you. Make a jeweled box for it. Don't take it as wisdom but only as information. Consciously make a box for it. Then gradually you will find, as experiences begin happening, that my words arise from your unconscious, and make clear and comprehensible the experiences that happen.

For an experiment, simply try to hold air in your hand. As soon as you tighten your grip the air escapes. The tighter you clench your fist, the less air you hold, until in the end there is no air left. Loose your grip and air will rush toward your open hand. There is always air in an open hand, but from the closed fist it flees. One who keeps his hand open has it always full of air; it is never empty, every moment the air is fresh. Have you ever observed this? An open hand is never empty, and a closed hand is always empty; and if a little air remains in the closed fist, it is stale and old and decayed.

They alone are able to enjoy who renounce. In this world, in this life, man gets as much as he is willing to give up and let go. This is paradoxical—but all the rules of life are paradoxical.

It is sheer stupidity to hold on to anything in life. The great mistake is to grasp tightly; in doing so one loses what one would have got. In claiming that "it is mine," we lose what is ours already.

XVII. Silence

When you go in, you touch a new kind of silence—the presence of silence itself.

It is not only an absence of noise, it is something absolutely positive, almost visible, tangible.

Even the profound silence to be found amongst the trees is nothing compared to the inner silence. The outer, however profound it is, remains shallow; it has no depth. One can go into a forest, one can go into the mountains—there is certainly silence, but it is in fact a negative silence. The marketplace and its noise are not there, the traffic noise is not there. The airplane passing by, the train, the people and the dogs barking, are not there. It is the absence of noise; hence it cannot be profound.

When you go in, you touch a new kind of silence—the presence of silence itself. It is not only an absence of noise, it is something absolutely positive, almost visible, tangible—and that is the difference. The outer silence can be disturbed any moment, but the inner silence can never be disturbed. No noise can ever penetrate it. And once you have felt it, even in the marketplace you will remain silent. It becomes an undercurrent. On the surface you may be involved in activities, in working, but deep down it is all silent. Nothing disturbs it, nothing distracts you from it; you remain rooted in it.

For thousands of years the monks, the nuns, have been leaving the world in search of silence. Of course they find a certain silence in the jungles and forests, in the monasteries—but that is just an absence of noise, it is not true silence.

True silence can only be found when you move inwards. It exists in your very interiority. Then it has infinite depth and infinite height. It is immeasurable. And to know it is to know all.

There are very few people who love silence, although many people say they would like to be silent. But the moment they are silent they are not happy; they start immediately searching for some diversion, distraction, some occupation. They are afraid of being silent and there is a reason why they are afraid—because the more silent you become the more you disappear.

You are noise because you are your mind, you are noise because you are your ego. When the mind disappears, the mind and the ego both start evaporating. Then there is silence. Then you are really close to your authentic center, but you are unaware of it so you don't know where you are going. It seems like you are falling into an abysmal depth, a bottomless phenomenon. Fear grips you and you start searching for some diversion, some occupation—anything to cling to.

And these are the people who hanker for immortality—and they don't know what to do on their off day! Just think: if they are really allowed to be immortals, what will they do? People talk about beautiful things, not knowing what they are talking about.

But if one loves silence then one loves existence, then one loves truth. Then one loves religion in its purest essence, because it is only through silence that one discovers the scriptures—scriptures that are hidden within you, sermons that are ready to explode within you, light that is waiting and waiting for you to come home. To love silence is what *sannyas* is all about. *Sannyas* can be defined as a tremendous love for silence.

XVIII. Past Lives

One dream comes, is followed by another dream, and is followed by yet another dream. The pilgrim starts from one moment and enters into the next one. Moment after moment, the moments keep disappearing, but the pilgrim continues moving on.

My suggestion is, don't ask whether the theory of reincarnation is true or not. To me it is true, to you it is not—not yet. Don't take any position, negative or positive. Just remain open to the hypothesis. Explore. If you can go into your own past lives, that's enough proof that everybody has a long, long past. And that gives another insight: if there are past lives, that means there are going to be future lives; this life is only just in the middle. Of course, to enter future lives is not possible because the future has not happened yet. But to enter the past is absolutely easy because it has already happened; the memory is there and the record is there. It is just that you have forgotten the way to the record room where it is kept.

Take it as a hypothesis. With me, everything is a hypothesis. If you can trust only this much, that you are ready to explore, inquire, that will do.

I have no doctrines to teach you, but only methods for you to find out the truth by yourself. Any truth that is not found by you is not truth. Truth is truth only when *you* have found it.

When you lie down to sleep at night—when sleep begins to descend upon you and has almost caught you—bring your consciousness to the last thought in your mind, then go to sleep; and when you wake up in the morning and are ready to leave your bed, look back and find your first thought on waking. You will be very surprised by the result. The last thought of the night becomes the first one in the morning. In the same way, the last desire at the time of death becomes the first desire at the time of birth.

In death, the body disintegrates but the mind continues its journey. The age of your body may be fifty years but that of your mind can be five million. The sum total of all the minds born in all your births is there in you even today. Buddha has given a very significant name to this happening. He was the first to do so. He named it the "storehouse of consciousness". Like a storehouse, your mind has stored all the memories of all your past births—so your mind is very old. And it is not that your mind is the storehouse of only human births: if you were born as animals or as trees, as is surely the case, the memories of all those births are also present within you.

People who have conducted profound inquiries into the storehouse of consciousness say that if all of a sudden the feeling of love swells in someone on seeing a rose, the reason is that there is a memory deep within that person of being a rose in the past, which is rekindled on feeling its resonance in a rose. It is not accidental if a person loves dogs very much. There are memories in his storehouse of consciousness that make him aware of his great kinship with dogs. Whatever happens in our lives is not accidental. A subtle process of cause and effect is working behind these happenings.

"Who am I?" is a very fundamental question, and a very existential question at that. "Who am I?" is a question which involves the totality of our existence in all its depth and heights. This question will take me where I was before I was ever born, behind all my past lives. This question can take me where I was in the primeval beginning. The profoundness of this question is infinite. And so is its journey equally profound.

XIX. Innocence

If you really want to know, you will have to drop all your knowledge; you will have to unlearn it.
You will have to become ignorant again, like a small child with wondering eyes, with alertness.

Buddha himself is not very knowledgeable; neither is Jesus, nor is Mohammed. They are innocent people, simple people, but their simplicity is such, their innocence is such, their childlike quality is such that they have been able to penetrate into the innermost core of their beings. They have been able to know their truth; they have been able to reach the very core of their existence. They know, but they are not knowledgeable. Their knowing is not through scriptures. Their knowing has happened through watchfulness. Remember the source: real knowing comes through meditation, awareness, consciousness, mindfulness, watchfulness, witnessing. And unreal knowledge comes through scriptures. You can learn the unreal knowledge very easily and you can brag about it, but you will remain a fool—a learned fool, but a fool all the same.

If you really want to know, you will have to drop all your knowledge, you will have to unlearn it. You will have to become ignorant again, like a small child, with wondering eyes, with alertness. You will be able to know not only your own being but also the being that exists in the world . . . the being that exists in the trees and the birds and the animals and the rocks and the stars. If you are able to know yourself, you will be able to know all that is.

Innocence is your very nature. You do not have to become it, you are already it. You are born innocent. Then layers and layers of conditioning are imposed upon your innocence. Your innocence is like a mirror and conditioning is like layers of dust. The mirror has not to be achieved, the mirror is already there—or rather, here. The mirror is not lost, it is only hidden behind the layers of dust.

You don't have to follow a path to reach your nature because you cannot leave your nature, you cannot go anywhere else. Even if you wanted to, it is impossible. That's exactly the definition of nature: nature means that which cannot be left behind, that which cannot be renounced. But you can forget about it—you cannot lose it, but it can be forgotten. And that's exactly what has happened. The mirror is not lost but forgotten—forgotten because it is not functioning anymore as a mirror. Not that any defect has arisen in it, just layers of dust are covering it. All that is needed is to clean it, to remove those layers of dust.

The process of becoming innocent is not really a process of becoming, it is a process of discovering your being. It is a discovery, not an achievement. You don't attain to something new, you simply attain to that which you have always been. It is a forgotten language.

It happens many times: you see a person on the road, you recognize him, his face seems familiar. Suddenly you remember also that you know his name. You say, "It is just on the tip of my tongue," but still it is not coming to you. What is happening? If it is just on the tip of your tongue, then why can't you say it? You know that you know it, but still you are not able to remember it. And the more you try, the more difficult it becomes, because making an effort makes you more tense. And when you are tense, you are farther away from your nature; you are farther away from that which is already there. When you are relaxed you are closer; when you are utterly relaxed, it will surface of its own accord.

So you try hard, but it doesn't come, so you forget all about it. Then lying down in your bath, or just swimming in the pool—you are not even trying to remember that man's name—when suddenly it bubbles up. What has happened? You were not trying to remember, and you were relaxed. When you are relaxed you are wide, when you are tense you become narrow—the more tense, the more narrow. The passage between you and that which is inside you becomes so narrow that nothing can pass through it, not even a single name.

All the great scientific discoveries have been made in this very mysterious way—in this very unscientific way, so to speak. Once you have dropped the effort you become relaxed, you become restful. You become soft, you become wide, you become open. It is there inside, it surfaces. Finding the mind no longer tense, it surfaces.

Innocence is there, you have simply forgotten it—you have been made to forget it. Society is cunning. For centuries man has learned that you can survive in this society only if you are cunning; the more cunning you are, the more successful you will be. That's the whole game of politics: be cunning, be more cunning than others. It is a constant struggle and competition as to who can be more cunning. Whoever is more cunning is going to succeed, is going to be powerful.

After centuries of cunningness man has learned one thing: that to remain innocent is dangerous, you will not be able to survive. Hence parents try to drive their children out of their innocence. Teachers, schools, colleges, universities exist for the simple work of making you more cunning, more clever. Although they call it intelligence, it is not intelligence. Intelligence is not against innocence, remember. Intelligence is the flavor of innocence; intelligence is the fragrance of innocence.

And innocence has not to be achieved; it is already there. It has only to be discovered—or rediscovered. You have to drop all that you have learned from others, and you will immediately be innocent.

Don't just go on living on borrowed information. Start seeking and searching for your own intelligence. A negative process is needed; it is to be achieved through *via negativa*. You have to negate all that has been given to you. You have to say, "This is not mine; hence I have no claim over it. It may be true, it may not be true. Who knows? Others say it is so, but unless it becomes my experience I cannot agree or disagree.

I will not believe or disbelieve. I will not be a Catholic or a communist, I will not be a Hindu or a Mohammedan. I will simply not follow any ideology." Because whomever you follow, you will be gathering dust around yourself.

Just drop all knowledge. It hurts because you have carried that knowledge for so long and you have been bragging so much about that knowledge—your degrees, M.A.s and Ph.Ds, and you have been bragging about all those degrees. And suddenly I am saying to drop all that nonsense?

Just be as simple as a child. Just be again a child as you were born, as you came into this world. In that mirrorlike state you will be able to reflect that which is. Innocence is the door to knowing. Knowledge is the barrier and innocence is the bridge.

XX. Beyond Illusion

BEYOND ILLUSION

It takes a little effort to get out of illusions because we have invested in them very much. They are our hopes: It is through them that we go on living.

The mind lives in illusions. The mind is nothing but all the illusions accumulated in you: illusions as memories, illusions as imagination, illusions as dreams, hopes, desires. And in the very center of all these illusions is the illusion of "I am"—the ego. That is the very root, the central illusion, and all other illusions move around it. They support it, they feed it, they are supported by it and they are fed by it; it is a mutual arrangement. And between these two, you and your reality are utterly lost.

Meditation simply means getting out of this illusory state—of dreams, desires, past, future—and just being in the moment that surrounds you. Just to be utterly in the moment, with no thought, is to be in reality. It takes a little effort to drop out of the illusions because we have lived in those illusions for so long; it has become almost habitual, a second nature. It also takes a little effort to get out of those illusions because we have invested in them very much. They are our hopes: it is through them that we go on living, prolonging. To drop them means to drop the future, to drop all hopes; and we don't know how to live in the present without hope.

That is the whole art: to live in the present and without hope. And remember, living without hope does not mean living hopelessly. Living without hope simply means that the present is so tremendously beautiful, who cares about the future? Who bothers about it? Not that one is living in despair and hopelessness, but that one is so fulfilled in the present that there is no space left to think about the future.

The person who lives in hopelessness lives an empty life. He does not know what the present is, and the future has disappeared. He was only living for the future, the carrot that goes on hanging there— "tomorrow"—and never arrives. One goes on working hard to catch the carrot. Because it is never caught, one goes on running after it. Ultimately death takes you, and still you have not arrived. This is the story of millions of people. They live in hope without any fulfillment ever, and they die unfulfilled.

To live without hope simply means to live here, now, knowing that there is no tomorrow; it is always today. Then a totally different kind of life starts getting crystallized in you. It is so utterly joyous that one does not think of the past and one does not think of the future.

We think of the past and the future only because the present is very empty, because we don't know how to live this moment. So either we run towards the past or we run towards the future, which is in a way the same. The past is no more, the future is not yet; both are nothings. Between these two nothings is this moment, and this moment is all.

The effort that we have been making in the East down through the centuries, is not to solve problems. For example, in your nightmare you try to solve the problem of what to do with this lion that is following you. That's what psychoanalysis is. Or you start trying to find out where it comes from, how it happened in the first place—"Why is this lion following me? And from where is this fear coming? And why am I climbing the tree?" And you meet somebody who is very expert in analyzing things, in explaining, in creating theories, in telling you how it happened in the first place. Maybe it is a birth trauma or maybe your parents have not treated you well. Or maybe this lion is somebody. Just look directly into its eyes—it is your wife or your husband, and you are afraid of your wife or your husband.

But all these explanations take one thing for granted—that it is real. And that is the basic problem, not where the lion has come from or what the symbolic meaning of the lion is. That is not the real problem. The real problem is whether or not the lion is real. Psychoanalysis does not help you to become aware that mind is an unreal thing—illusion, *maya*. In fact, it takes you more into the mud and the mire. It takes you deeper, to the roots. But an illusion cannot have any roots. You will always be getting to the roots but you will not arrive. An illusion cannot have any cause.

Now let me repeat it, because this will make the difference very clear. An illusion cannot have any cause, so you cannot search for the cause. You can go on and on, you can go into the unconscious of man . . . Freud did that, and did it perfectly, but that didn't solve anything. Jung had to go deeper. He had to find something like the collective unconscious. And you can go on. Then you can find the universal unconscious, and so on, so forth, layer upon layer. You can go on analyzing—that maybe it is a birth trauma, that you became very much afraid when you came out of the birth canal from your mother's womb. But things don't end there, because you were in your mother's womb for nine months. Those nine months cannot be simply dropped. In those nine months much happened to you. You have to go into analyzing that.

And if you go deep enough you will have to enter into your previous life—that's what Hindu analysts have done. They say "previous life," and then "previous to previous," and go on and on backwards. And you reach nowhere. Either way you come to a point where you see the whole futility of it.

To see the futility of the mind and to see that an illusion cannot have any cause and cannot be analyzed, the only thing that can be done is to make yourself a little bit alert, aware—in that very awareness the dream disappears. It has no grip over you. And once the mind is not there gripping you, you are a totally new person. A new consciousness is born in you.

XXI. Completion

Remember one basic law: anything that is complete drops, because then there is no meaning in carrying it; anything that is incomplete clings, it waits for its completion.

And this existence is really always longing for completion.

The whole existence has a basic tendency to complete everything. It does not like incomplete things—they hang, they wait; and there is no hurry for existence—they can wait for millions of years.

Do you remember anything that you have completed? Do you have any moment in your life, any experience, which you can say is complete, total? If you have any experience that is complete, the mind will never go back to it. There is no need. There is no need! It is absolutely useless. The mind simply tries to complete everything. The mind has a tendency to complete. And this is necessary; otherwise life will be impossible.

So the constant monologue that everybody carries within is really a part of wrong living—incomplete living. Nothing is finished, and you go on making new beginnings. Then the mind goes on becoming piled up with incomplete things. They will never be completed, but they will create a burden on the mind—a constant burden, a growing burden, an increasing burden—and that creates the monologue.

That is why the older you grow, the more the monologue grows with you. And old men begin to talk aloud. Really, the burden is so great that the control is lost. So look at old men. They will be sitting, and their legs will be working, and they will be talking, and they will be making gestures. What are they doing? You think they have gone crazy, that they are old and now they have become senile. No, that is not the case. They have had a long, incomplete life, and now death is coming nearer and mind is in haste, trying to complete everything. And it seems impossible!

So if you really want to break this monologue, which means silence, then try to complete everything that you are doing. And do not start new things—you will go crazy. Finish whatever you are doing, all the very small things.

You are taking a bath: Make it complete. How to make it complete? Be there! Your presence will do it. Be there, enjoy it, live it, feel it. Be sensitive to the water falling on you, be saturated. Come out of your bath doing it completely, totally. Otherwise the bath will follow you. It will become a shadow; it will go with you. You are eating—then eat! Then forget everything else; then let nothing exist in the world except your present act.

Whatever you are doing, do it so completely, so unhurriedly, so patiently that the mind is saturated and becomes content. Only then leave it. Three months of continuous awareness about doing each of your acts completely will give you some intervals in your monologue. Then, for the first time, you will become aware that the internal monologue is a by-product of incomplete living.

Buddha has used the term "right living." He has given an eight-fold path. In those eight principles, one is "right living." Right living means total living; wrong living means incomplete living.

If you are angry, then be really angry. Be authentically angry; make it complete. Suffer it! There is no harm in suffering because suffering brings much wisdom. There is no harm in suffering because only through suffering does one transcend it. Suffer it! But be authentically angry.

What are you doing? You are angry and you are smiling. Now the anger will follow you. You can deceive the whole world but you cannot deceive yourself, you cannot deceive your mind. The mind knows very well that the smile is false. Now anger will continue inside; that will become a monologue. Then whatever you have not said aloud, you will have to say within. Whatsoever you have not done, you will imagine doing. Now you will create a dream. You will fight with your enemy, with the object of your anger. The mind is trying to help you to complete a certain thing. But that too is impossible because you are doing other things.

Even this can be helpful: Close your room—you were not angry; the situation was such that you could not be—close your room and now be angry. But do not continue the monologue. Act it out! There is no necessity to act it out on a person, a pillow will do. Fight with the pillow, act out your anger, express it—but let it be authentic, real. Let it be real, and then you will feel a sudden relaxation inside. Then the monologue will drop, it will break. There will be an interval, a gap. That gap is silence.

So the first thing is to break the monologue. And you can do it only if your living becomes a "right living," a complete living. Never be incomplete. Live every moment as if there is no other moment to come. Then only will you complete it. Know that death can occur at any moment; this may be the last. Feel that, "If I have to do something, I must do it here and now, completely!"

The Master

THE MASTER

Once you have seen a buddha, an enlightened one, a tremendous flame suddenly starts blossoming in you. "If this beauty, this grace, this wisdom, this blissfulness can happen to any man, then why can it not happen to me?"

The master is nothing but a challenge: "If it has happened to me, it can happen to you." And the authentic master—there are so many teachers propounding doctrines, beliefs, philosophies—the authentic master is not concerned with words. He is not concerned with beliefs, atheism or theism, is not concerned even with God or heaven and hell. The authentic master is concerned only with one single thing—to provoke you to see your potentiality, to see inward. His presence makes you silent, his words deepen your silence, his very being slowly starts melting your falseness, your mask, your personality.

The master's function is to give you a taste of insecurity, to give you a taste of openness. And once you know that openness, that insecurity. . . . They are basic ingredients of freedom. Without them you cannot open your wings and fly in the sky of infinity.

It is absolutely essential to avoid the teachers; they are fake masters. It is very difficult, because they speak the same language. So you have not to listen to the words, you have to listen to the heart. You have not to listen to their doctrines, their logic and arguments, you have to listen to their grace, their beauty, their eyes. You have to listen to and feel the aura that surrounds a master. Just like a cool breeze it touches you. Once you have found a master, you have found a key to open the treasure of your potentialities.

To find a master is easy if you are available not only to words but to silences too; not only to words, because the truth never comes through words, but between the words, between the lines, in the silent spaces. If you are searching for a master, don't carry any criterion, any prejudice. Be absolutely available, so that when you come across a master you can feel his energy. He carries a whole world of energy around him. His own experience radiates all around him. If you are open and not afraid of experiencing a new thing, of tasting something original, it is not very difficult to find a master. What difficulty there is, is on your side.

The master is your future: that which you *can* become he *has* become. The master is nothing but your own unfoldment: you are a seed, he is a flower. Let the master become an invitation to you—the invitation for the inner spring, the invitation for the inner flower. The possibility is there, and unless that possibility becomes actual you will never be satisfied. Unless a person becomes a god there is no benediction, no bliss. And each person is a potential god, and the whole of life is a task to transform the potential into the actual.

THE SUIT OF FIRE
(WANDS)

Energy—Action—Response

William Blake is right when he says, "Energy is delight."
That's a very profound statement. Yes, energy is delight, and
the greater the energy you have the greater will be your
delight. Overflowing energy becomes celebration. When the
energy is dancing in you, in unison, in a deep harmony, in
rhythm and flow, you become a blessing to the world.

Energy

Life is a tremendous energy phenomenon. You are not aware of how
much energy you have. Do you think atoms know how much energy
they have? A single atom, which is invisible to the eyes, if it explodes,
can destroy a city as big as Hiroshima or Nagasaki. Within minutes
everything is burned. If an atom of matter has that much energy, just
think—your consciousness is a far higher phenomenon. Your being must
be carrying universes of energies—dormant, of course, because you are
not aware. But those who have become aware, their descriptions give an
indication.

Kabir says that in his experience of inner being, it is as if thousands of suns have suddenly arisen. All around him suns are dancing; the light is so dazzling that it makes him almost blind. But this is not only Kabir's experience. Many mystics have described it the same way.

But don't be worried; this energy is creative, not destructive. Any energy that comes out of meditative silence is creative. There is not a single instance of it destroying anything; it has only created. It has created a beautiful space within, and it has created beautiful art, music, sculpture, poetry, painting, outside. This fire is not even hot, it is very cool.

For example, the story of Moses—he went to Mount Sinai in search of God and he saw a fire, and within the fire a green bush, unburned. He could not believe his eyes. The flames were rising high and the bush inside the flames was green, and its flowers were blossoming as if a cool breeze was passing through, not a fire.

Theologians have been trying to figure it out. I am not a theologian, but I can understand a little bit of poetry and I think it is a poetic statement, not a theological statement. What is being said is that life is a cool energy, so creative, so non-destructive, that even within its fire, a bush will remain green and will grow and blossom.

Accept this life energy—create a communion with this life energy, a dialogue, and you will be immensely enriched, not burned. For the first time your spring will come and your flowers will blossom.

Rejoice with the flames of the energy, dance with those flames, have a communion with those flames and you will be finding a dialogue with existence itself. If you are afraid that you may be burned, then this very fear will stop the process, will become a barrier to entering inward into deeper realms of your consciousness. Drop this fear. Nobody has ever been burned by life energy.

One has to learn to drop fear as one enters inward—because there is nobody except your own energy, and your own energy cannot be your enemy. In fact even to say "your energy" is not right. It is because of the poverty of language that we have to use expressions like that. It is better to say you *are* the energy. Who is there to be burned? You are the fire itself, those dancing flames are your very being.

Action

Mind always thinks in terms of purpose, profit, utility. When the mind disappears, action does not disappear, *activity* disappears—and there is a great difference between the two. Activity has utility; action is pure joy, pure beauty. You act not because something has to be achieved; you act because action is a dance, is a song. You act because you are so full of energy.

Have you watched a child running on the sea beach? You ask him, "Why are you running? What is the purpose of your running? What are you going to gain out of it?" Have you watched the child collecting seashells on the beach? You ask him, "What is the utility of it all? You can use your time in a more utilitarian way. Why waste your time?"

The child is not concerned about utility at all; he is enjoying his energy. He is so full of energy, so bubbling with energy that it is a sheer dance—any excuse will do. These are just excuses—seashells, pebbles, colored stones. These are just excuses—the sun, the beautiful beach . . . just excuses to run and to jump and to shout with joy. There is no utility at all.

"Energy is delight"—that is a statement made by William Blake, one of the most mystical poets of the West. Energy *is* delight. When there is great energy, what are you going to do with it? It is bound to explode.

Action comes out of energy, out of delight. Activity is businesslike. Action is poetry; activity creates bondage because it is result oriented. You are doing it not for its own sake, you are doing it for some goal. There is a motive. And then there is frustration. Out of a hundred cases, ninety-nine times you will not achieve the goal, so ninety-nine times you will be in misery, frustration. You did not enjoy the activity itself, you were waiting for the result. Now the result has come, and ninety-nine times out of a hundred there is frustration. And don't hope for the remaining one percent, because when you achieve the goal, there is frustration also. The goal is achieved, but suddenly you realize that all the dreams you have been dreaming about the goal are not fulfilled.

Activity means there is a goal; activity is only a means to an end. Action means that the means and the end are together. That's the difference between action and activity.

When action arises in you, it has a totally different dimension. You act for the sheer joy of acting. Action is an end unto itself; it has no utility. When the mind disappears, with it all utilitarian activities will also disappear, because mind is the cause of goal orientation. It contains all your motives. It contains your past and the future; it does not contain the present at all. And when there is no mind, all that is left is pure present. You act moment to moment, and each moment is enough unto itself.

Response

Action means response; activity means reaction. When you are in action, it means the mind is put aside and your consciousness is in a direct contact with existence; hence the response is immediate. Then whatsoever you do is not ready-made. It is not a ready-made answer given by the mind; you are responding to the reality as it is. Then there is beauty, because your action is true to the situation.

But millions of people in the world are simply living through ready-made answers. They are already carrying the answer; they don't listen, they don't see the situation confronting them. They are more interested in the answer that they are carrying within themselves than in the question itself, and they go on living their answer again and again. That's why their life becomes repetitive, boring, a drag. It is no longer a dance, it cannot be a dance.

Action is a dance; activity is a drag. Activity is always untrue to the situation; action is always true to the situation. And activity is always inadequate because it carries an answer from the past, and life goes on changing every moment, so whatsoever you bring from the past is never adequate, it always falls short. So whatsoever you do, there is frustration; you feel that you have not been able to cope with reality. You always feel something is missing, you always feel your reaction was not exactly as it should have been. And the reason is that you have simply repeated, parrotlike, a ready-made answer, cheap but untrue—untrue because the situation is new.

Action means there is no goal to it. Just as the poets say "poetry for poetry's sake" or "art for art's sake," the same is the situation with the mystic. His action is for action's sake; there is no other goal to it. He enjoys it just like a small child; innocently he enjoys it.

King of Fire: The Creator

THE CREATOR

The creator's joy is in creation itself; there is no other reward.

The only virtue worth calling virtue is creativity. What you create does not matter, but it should enhance life, beautify existence, make living more joyous, the song a little more juicy, the love a little more glorious—and the life of a creator starts becoming part of eternity and immortality.

Millions of people live, but they don't create anything. And it is one of the fundamentals of life that unless you create—it may be a painting, a song, a dance—you cannot be blissful, you will remain in misery. Only creativity brings to you your dignity. It helps you to blossom in your fullness.

The creator cannot be part of the crowd. The creator has to learn to be alone, to go apart, to learn the beauty of solitude, because only in that space does your potential start changing into actuality. The way of the creator ultimately leads you to yourself, because you are going away from the crowd, away from the mass—you are going into aloneness. A painter is absolutely alone in his vision. A dancer is absolutely alone in his dance.

One of the great dancers, Nijinsky, was asked once, "You dance before big audiences—don't you feel nervous?" He said, "As far as I am concerned, I feel nervous, but only to the point before the dance starts. Once I am in my dance I am absolutely alone, there is nobody else. Not only do others disappear, a moment comes sometimes—and that is the greatest moment—when I myself disappear and only the dance remains."

This has been observed about Nijinsky by scientists, that there were some moments when he would jump so high that it was not physically possible because of gravitation. And more amazing was the part when he would come down. He would come down so slowly— just as if a leaf is falling slowly towards the earth; there is no hurry. That, too, gravitation does not allow; gravitation pulls things forcibly.

He was asked about this and he said, "It is a mystery to me. Whenever I try, it never happens, because *I* am there. Perhaps I am the weight on which gravity works. When I forget myself completely, suddenly it is there—I am just a watcher as you are a watcher, full of wonder. I don't know how it happens."

Perhaps the ego is the heaviest thing in you. In the moment when Nijinsky felt that he himself had disappeared—only the dance was there, the dancer no more—he touched on the same experience as Gautam Buddha or Lao Tzu, but from a very different dimension. His dance became a mystic experience.

The creator's joy is in creation itself; there is no other reward. And the moment you start thinking of any reward beyond your act, you are only a technician, not a creator.

The creator is not ambitious and he is not lusting for eminence.

Those who are ambitious and who are lusting for eminence are only third-rate people. They may be composers, but they are not creators. A creator has no intention of being famous, has no intention of being respectable. His whole energy is involved in only one thing: his creation.

All the old, great pieces of art . . . for example, we don't know who was the architect of the Taj Mahal, the most beautiful architecture in the whole world. We don't know who created the *Upanishads*, the most beautiful statements about the ultimate experiences of man. They thought themselves simply vehicles, mediums of existence, only instrumental to the creativity of existence—they never thought that they were the creators. It is ugly even to sign your name.

And you see the masses . . . they have not created anything, but in every public toilet they have signed; in movie houses they have engraved their names on the seats. Such a desire that your name should remain after you are gone, such a desire to be eminent, to be ambitious, is not part of a creative soul, it is part of the mundane and the mediocre.

Queen of Fire: Sharing

The more you share, the more you will have. In the ordinary economics you share and you lose; in the spiritual economics you share and you get more.

In ordinary economics you have to be a miser, then only can you become rich . . . accumulate, never share. In the spiritual economics, if you are a miser whatever you have will be lost. It can live only if you share; it is a living experience. By sharing it continues a dynamic movement.

I have heard about a young man who had just received a great lottery prize, and he was immensely pleased. He stopped his car because a beggar was standing there. The beggar had been standing there every day, but he had never stopped his car. But today was different. The young man gave him a hundred-dollar bill. The beggar laughed.

The man said, "I don't understand. Why are you laughing?"

He said, "It reminds me . . . once I used to have my own car and I used to be just as generous as you are. I am laughing because soon you will be standing by my side. Don't be so generous! Learn something from my experience."

In the ordinary economics, the moment you give something, you have that much less. But have you felt that by giving love you have less love? Or by sharing your joy, have you felt that your joy is a little bit less? If you have watched, you will be surprised: by sharing, your joy is a little bit more; by loving, your sources of love are flowing more— you are juicier. By dancing . . . just to share yourself with your friends, you will not find yourself losing something, but gaining something.

Don't listen to the advice of other people. They know only about the ordinary economics. They don't know anything about a higher economics, where giving is sharing and where not giving is very destructive.

The more you give, the more you will have, the less you give, the less you will have. And if you don't give at all, you will not have anything at all.

Give with more totality, without any hesitation, and without holding anything back. Don't listen to others. Listen to your own experience; watch your own experience—when you give, do you lose something or do you gain something? That should be the decisive thing.

Knight of Fire: Intensity

If you live totally, intensely, then you are free, you have lived the moment and it is finished. You don't look back and you don't look ahead, you simply remain here now.

If you are just lukewarm in your search, then the ultimate is very far away from you. If you are total in your thirst and nothing is being held back—you have taken a jump into it, you have not left anything behind, no part of you is missing; you have jumped as a whole organic unity with your anger, your love, your hate, your greed, all together; you have staked whatsoever you have, whatsoever nature has given you—then the distance is almost nil.

It depends on your intensity. The proportion of your intensity will decide the proportion of the distance between godliness and your ungodly sleep.

Have you watched it, that whenever you are intense in anything the self disappears? You are in love with someone—in the very intensity of your love, the self disappears. You are no more, there is only love. Or you are in anger—in the intensity and totality of anger, the self disappears. You are no longer there, only the anger exists.

You can watch it in your own life. Whenever something is there, possessing you all in all, the self is not found. That is a great clue. The self is there only when you are half-hearted in something. That which you hold back becomes the self.

If you are totally involved in painting, in doing some work, singing a song or dancing or playing guitar, if you are totally in it, you will immediately see you are not there. Something of the beyond has taken possession of you. The self is not there, unself is.

And you have come to this point many times, unawares of course.

Seeing a beautiful sunset, you were so lost in the beauty of it that for a moment there was no idea of the self. You were not there. There was a totally different quality: you were not there. Something was there, but you cannot call it "I," you cannot call it any frozen state of the ego. You were fluid, flowing.

This is what Krishnamurti calls the moment when the observer becomes the observed. The sunset was there and the sunset was too much. It possessed you. The observer disappeared into the observed. The sunset was all; you were not separate, you were not standing aloof and watching, you were not a spectator. You were in it, you were part of it. You started feeling a kind of melting, merging.

Hence the liberating experience of beauty; hence the liberating experience of love; hence the liberating experience of music, great music. These moments you have known—they come naturally, and they go. But you have never been able to reduce them to a scientific approach. You have not meditated over them, you have not looked into the keys that are hidden in them.

Just look at a child of three and you will see what liveliness should be, how joyous he is and how sensitive to everything that goes on happening around him, how alert, watchful; nothing misses his eye. And how intense in everything: if he is angry, he is just anger, pure anger. It is beautiful to see a child in anger, because old people are always half-hearted, even if they are angry they are not totally in it, they are holding back. They don't love totally, they are not angry totally, they don't do anything in totality, they are always calculating. Their life has become lukewarm. It never comes to that intensity of one hundred degrees where things evaporate, where something happens, where revolution becomes possible.

But a child always lives at one hundred degrees—whatsoever he does. If he hates you he hates you totally, and when he loves you he loves you totally; and in a single moment he can change. He is so quick! He does not take time, he does not brood over it. Just one moment before, he was sitting in your lap and telling you how much he loves you. And then something happens—you say something and something goes wrong between you and him—and he jumps out of your lap and says, "I never want to see you again." And see in his eyes the totality of it!

And because it is total, it does not leave a trace behind. That's the beauty of totality: it does not accumulate psychological memory. Only partial living creates psychological memory. Then everything that you have lived only in part hangs around you, and the hangover continues for your whole life. Thousands of things are hanging there unfinished.

That's the whole theory of karma: unfinished jobs, unfinished actions go on waiting to be finished, to be completed, and they go on goading you: "Complete me!" Because every action wants to be fulfilled. . . .

But if you live totally, intensely, then you are free of it, you have lived the moment and it is finished. You don't look back and you don't look ahead, you simply remain here now. There is no past, no future. That's what I mean by celebration. In a real moment of celebration only the present exists.

Page of Fire: Playfulness

Play is something in which a goal is not at all involved. The very being together is beautiful—for the sheer joy of it! In a better world, with more understanding, games will disappear; there will only be play.

There cannot be any map to the land of playfulness. All maps lead to seriousness. Playfulness is when all maps have been burned. There is no way to playfulness, because playfulness is not a goal and cannot be a goal. When you forget about goals, when you are not going anywhere, when the very idea of going is dropped, then here-now playfulness starts growing in you, happening in you.

Playfulness is not then and there; it is here, now. So how can there be a road map? You are not to go anywhere, you are just to be.

Seriousness is goal-oriented. And when a serious person starts playing, he even transforms the quality of the play—it becomes a game; it is no longer play. That is the difference between a game and play. When play becomes serious, it becomes a game.

People go to see wrestling, people go to see bullfights or American football—ugly, violent, inhuman. The people who are going to see these things are immature, and a little perverted too. The spectators are as ungrown-up as the gladiators. And both are in some way catharting; in the name of the game they are throwing their rubbish, they are simply vomiting their violence.

This is a very violent, violent world. That's why love cannot exist here. When human beings really become human beings, things like bullfighting and wrestling will be unheard of, they will become part of history. Just to imagine that thousands of people have come to see a bullfight looks so ugly, disgusting. But people are serious. They change play also into seriousness.

Play is something in which a goal is not at all involved. The very being together is beautiful—for the sheer joy of it! In a better world, with more understanding, games will disappear; there will only be play. There will be nobody as a winner, nobody as the defeated—because the very idea of defeating and winning is inhuman. There is no need for it! Why can't we enjoy the sheer togetherness? There should be no counting, no marking. There should not be any result out of it.

If you are in love with playing football, play football—just play it! Don't look for the result. If the result comes in, you become serious. The play is destroyed; it has become almost businesslike. Enjoy the sheer outpouring of energy, enjoy the moment—don't sacrifice it for anything else.

Ace of Fire: The Source

When the energy is just there—not going anywhere, just pulsating at the original source, just radiating its light there, blossoming like a lotus, neither going out nor going in—it is simply here and now.

When I say go inward, I am simply saying don't go on moving in the head. The whole society forces your energy to move in the head. All education consists of the basic techniques for how to pulsate the energy only in the head—how to make you a great mathematician, how to make you a great physician. All the education in the world consists of taking the energy into the head.

Zen asks you to come out of the head and go to the basic source—the place from where the educational system around the world has been taking the energy, putting it into the head, and turning it into thoughts, images, and creating thinking. The head has its uses. It is not that Zen is not aware of the uses of energy in the head, but if all the energy is used in the head, you will never become aware of your eternity. You may become a very great thinker and philosopher, but you will never know, as an experience, what life is. You will never know, as an experience, what it is to be one with the whole.

When the energy is just at the center, pulsating. . . . When it is not moving anywhere, neither in the head nor in the heart but at the very source from where the heart takes it, the head takes it . . . pulsating at the very source—that is the very meaning of Zazen.

Zazen means just sitting at the very source, not moving anywhere. A tremendous force arises, a transformation of energy into light and love, into greater life, into compassion, into creativity. It can take many forms, but first you have to learn how to be at the source. Then the source will decide where your potential is. You can relax at the source, and it will take you to your very potential. It does not mean that you have to stop thinking forever, it simply means you should be aware and alert and capable of moving into the source. When you need the head you can move the energy into the head, and when you need to love, you can move the energy into the heart.

But you need not think twenty-four hours. When you are not thinking you have to relax back into your center—that keeps you constantly content, alert, joyful. A blissfulness surrounds you; it is not an act, it is simply radiation.

Zazen is the strategy of Zen. Literally it means just sitting. Sitting where? Sitting at the very source.

❋

The source of luminosity is within you. It is not outside you. If you seek it outside, you seek in vain. Close your eyes and go within yourself. It is there . . . waiting since eternity. It is your innermost nature. You are luminosity, your being is luminous. This luminosity is not borrowed, it is your innermost core. It is you.

You are light—a light unto yourself.

2 of Fire: Possibilities

To live means to live dangerously; to live means to remain available to all possibilities. And infinite are the possibilities. You are not limited to any possibility, you have an unlimited being, unbounded. You can be anything; the next moment can bring anything.

Deep down, each individual is a whole humanity—not only a whole humanity, a whole existence. The tree exists in you, the dog exists in you, the tiger exists in you; the whole past exists in you and also the whole future. In a very atomic way, all that has happened in the world and all that is going to happen exists in you potentially. You can be in millions of ways, hence to live means to live dangerously, to live means to live through change, movement. One remains a river.

If you are secure, you become a pool of water; there will be no movement, no dynamism. Static, stagnant, the pool of water becomes dirty, and by and by it dies. A river is alive and nobody knows what will happen. It may get lost in a desert. What is going to happen is unpredictable. A predictable life is a mechanical life; unpredictable and you are throbbing with life, pulsating, vibrating. Then the whole lives through you.

✺

Nature is a culmination of infinite possibilities. Within these possibilities the heating of water to a hundred degrees centigrade is a natural happening, and the freezing of water at zero is also a natural happening. A natural phenomenon such as the freezing of water at zero does not negate the natural phenomenon of water turning into vapor at a hundred degrees. It is not that one event is natural while the other is not—both are natural.

Darkness is natural and so is light. Falling down is natural and so is rising up. There are infinite possibilities in nature. We are always standing on the crossroads from where an infinite number of paths emerge. And the interesting thing is that whatever we choose, the capability to choose will itself be a gift from nature. Even if we were to choose a wrong path, nature will bring us to the very end of it.

Nature is very cooperative. If we choose the road to hell, nature begins to clear the way and invites us to proceed. It will not stop you. Why would nature stop you from turning water into ice, if you wish to do so, and have you rather turn it into vapor? Nature will be happy to clear your way if you wish to go to hell, or to heaven. Whether you wish to live or die, nature will always be willing to cooperate. To live is natural, to die is natural, and your ability to choose either of the two is natural too. If you can grasp this multidimensionality of nature, you will have no difficulty in understanding what I am saying.

Suffering is natural and so is happiness. To live like a blind man is natural, and to live with open eyes is natural too. To be awake is natural, and to stay asleep is natural as well. Nature contains endless possibilities. And the interesting thing is that we are not living outside of nature, we are part of nature. Our choosing is also due to the natural capability we have within us.

As the individual becomes more and more conscious, his ability to choose becomes more and more profound. The more unconscious an individual is, the less profound is his ability to choose.

For example, there is no way that water lying in the sun cannot turn into vapor—it would be difficult for it not to. The water can't decide whether to become vapor or not. If it stays in the sun then it is sure to become vapor, and lying in the cold it is sure to become ice. This the water will have to live through, although it will have no knowledge that it is living through it because its consciousness is low, or not at all, or dormant.

Man faces much greater choices because his consciousness is much more evolved. He chooses not only through his body, he chooses through his mind as well. He not only chooses to travel on earth, he also chooses to travel vertically, in space. That too is within his power to choose.

Although this area has not been researched yet, I feel that in the near future science may discover there are trees that have suicidal tendencies—trees who may not be choosing to live, who may be wanting to stay short in the dense forest and eventually die. This is yet to be discovered.

Among human beings we can see clearly that there are people who are suicidal—they don't choose to live; they keep looking for ways of dying. Wherever they see a thorn, they rush towards it like a madman; flowers don't appeal to them. Wherever they see defeat they are drawn towards it as if hypnotized, but when they see victory they look for scores of excuses. People find thousands of arguments against the possibility of growth, but where they are certain of decay they keep moving head-on in that direction.

All choices are open to human beings. The more conscious a person becomes, the more his choices will lead him towards happiness; the more unconscious he is, the closer he will move towards misery.

3 of Fire: Experiencing

Sitting by a flower, don't be a man or a woman, be a flower. Sitting by a tree, don't be a man or a woman, be a tree. Taking a bath in a river, don't be a person, be a river. And then millions of signs are given to you.

Look! See! Feel! Touch! But don't think. The moment thinking enters, you are thrown off the track—then you live in a private world. Thinking is a private world; it belongs to you. Then you are enclosed, encapsulated, imprisoned within yourself. Non-thinking, you are no more. You are enclosed no more. Non-thinking, you open, you become porous; existence flows in you and you flow into existence.

But the tendency of the mind is to interpret. Before you see something you have already interpreted it. Even before I have said anything you are already thinking about it. That's how listening becomes impossible.

You will have to learn to listen. Listening means you are open, vulnerable, receptive, but you are not in any way thinking. Thinking is a positive action. Listening is passivity: you become like a valley and receive; you become like a womb and you receive. If you can listen, then nature speaks—but it is not a language. Nature doesn't use words. Then what does nature use? It uses signs. A flower is there: what is the sign in it? It is not saying anything, but can you say it is not saying anything really? It is saying much, but it is not using any words—a wordless message.

To hear the wordless you will have to become wordless, because only the same can hear the same, only the same can relate to the same.

Sitting by a flower, don't be a man or a woman, be a flower. Sitting by a tree, don't be a man or a woman, be tree. Taking a bath in a river, don't be a person, be a river. And then millions of signs are given to you. And it is not a communication—it is a communion. Then nature speaks, speaks in thousands of tongues, but not in language. It speaks from millions of directions, but you cannot consult a dictionary about it and you cannot ask a philosopher what it means. The moment you start thinking what it means you are already on the path of going astray.

Existence opens millions of doors for you, but you stand outside and you would like to know something about it from the outside. There is no outside in nature.

I would like to repeat these words: There is no outside to nature. Everything is inside.

4 of Fire: Participation

Jump into the river, that is the only way to know life. Jump into the river. Never be a spectator. The spectator is the poorest person in the world.

Life can be known only through participation. Don't be a spectator. The whole modern world has become just a spectator, a crowd of lookers-on. Somebody dances, you look at it. What are you doing? How can you look at a dance? A dance has to be felt, a dance has to be danced. Somebody is singing and you look and you listen. To know the song and the beauty of it you have to sing, you have to participate. But this calamity has taken epidemic proportions. You go on looking at everything.

You rush to the movie—for what? Can't you live a beautiful life? Why do you have to go to see a movie? People are glued to their chairs in front of their TVs just looking at other people's living. And they are not even living, they are acting for you. They are acting for you and you are seeing those actors—and nobody is living. The dancer is not a true dancer, he is a professional and you are the audience. All is false.

Look for the essential. When you start looking for the essential you will become a participant. You will know. A dance has to be known in only one way—that is to dance.

How can you know what swimming is if you just stand on the bank and watch somebody swimming? You will see the strokes and you will see the man doing something in the water . . . but how will you know the thrill that is happening to him, the kick that is happening to him, the sensation, the buoyancy, the joy? The feeling of the river, flowing with the river, dancing with the river—how will you know it by standing on the bank?

Jump into the river, that is the only way to know life. Jump into the river. Never be a spectator. The spectator is the poorest man in the world. Participate.

This is my feeling: that if there is any God, he is not going to ask you what right things you have done and what bad things you have done; what sins you committed and what virtues you followed, no. If there is any God, he is going to ask: Has your life been a celebration or a sadness? That's the only thing that can be asked.

When the whole existence celebrates, why are you standing separate, alone, isolated? And then you feel that you are a stranger. When flowers flower, why do you stand aloof? Why not flower? When birds sing, why do you stand aloof? Why not sing, why not become a participant?

5 of Fire: Totality

Always do whatever you want to do, but do it totally.

If it is good it will become part of you. If it is not good, you will come out of it. That is the beauty of being total . . . that is the secret of being total.

I don't say don't commit a sin. I have no commandments. I don't say, "Do this. This is moral and virtuous"—nothing like that. I say whatever you want to do, do. If you want to be a thief, be a total thief. If it is virtue it will become part of you. If it is not virtue you will come out of it. If you want to be angry, be totally angry. If it is worthwhile you will enjoy it. If you feel it is simply nonsense, it will simply drop of its own accord.

Totality is the criterion.

There is never any repentance in a buddha. He never looks back; there is no point. Each thing that he has done, he has done totally and perfectly.

You always have to look back for the simple reason that you are always partial, fragmentary. Only a part of your being gets involved, and you do everything in such a way that you are never wholly in it. Later on you start thinking, "I should have done that," or "I should have done this," or "Maybe a better way of doing it was possible." You start repenting, you start feeling guilty. Your actions are so incomplete, that's why there is this hang-up.

When some action is done with your totality, when you are entirely in it, then once you are out of it, you are entirely out of it.

Remember this fundamental law: if you are totally into something, you can be totally out of it. If you are not totally in it you will remain involved in it even when the time is past; even when its days are gone you will remain involved in it. Some part of you will go on clinging to the past, and you will always feel miserable. Whatever you choose, misery is bound to follow, because sooner or later you will realize that you could have done better.

But a person of awareness knows that there is no possibility of doing it any better. Then what is the point of remembering it? A buddha does not remember the past. Not that he has no memory—he has a clearer memory than you have—but that memory is just a silent storage. If he needs it, that memory can be used, but he is not a slave to the memory.

And he never thinks of the future. He never rehearses for the future, because he knows that "Whatever happens, I will always be there with my totality. More than that is not possible." So he simply acts spontaneously, with no memory, with no future projection. His act is total and of the present—and the act that is total and of the present brings freedom.

6 of Fire: Success

Just go on moving, enjoying whatsoever becomes available. If success is there, enjoy it. If failure is there, enjoy it—because failure brings a few enjoyments that no success can ever bring. Success also brings a few joys that no failure can ever bring.

If you want to be successful then you will remain miserable. You may succeed, you may not succeed; but one thing is certain: you will remain miserable.

If you want to succeed, and you succeed by chance, by coincidence, it is not going to fulfill you—because this is the way of the mind. Whatsoever you have got becomes meaningless, and the mind starts going ahead of you. It desires more and more and more—the mind is nothing but the desire for more. And this desire can never be fulfilled, because whatsoever you have got you can always imagine more. And the distance between that "more" and that which you have got will remain constant.

This is one of the most constant things in human experience: everything changes, but the distance between that which you have and that which you would like to have remains constant.

Albert Einstein says: The speed of time remains constant—that is the only constant. And buddhas say: The speed of mind remains constant. And the truth is that mind and time are not two things—they are both the same; two names for the same thing.

So if you want to succeed, you may succeed, but you will not be content. And what is the meaning of a success if you are not content? And this, I say, is only coincidence that you may succeed; the greater possibility is that you will fail, because you are not chasing success alone—millions of people are chasing. In a country of six hundred million people only one person can be the prime minister—and six hundred million people are wanting to be the president or the prime minister. So only one succeeds, and the whole crowd fails. The greater possibility is that you will fail; mathematically that seems to be more certain than success.

If you fail you feel frustrated; your whole life seems to be a sheer wastage. If you succeed, you never succeed; if you fail, you fail—this is the whole game.

But if you are against success, then again you have another idea of being successful. That is, how to drop this nonsense of being successful. Then you have another idea . . . again the distance, again the desire.

Now, this is what makes people monks, makes people move into monasteries. They are against success. They want to go out of the world, where there is competition—they want to escape from it all so that there will be no provocation, no temptation; they can rest in themselves. And they try not to desire success—but this is a desire! Now they have an idea of spiritual success: how to succeed and become a buddha, how to succeed and become a Christ. Again an idea, again the distance, again the desire—again the whole game starts.

I am not against success; that's why I am in the world; otherwise I would have escaped. I am not for it, I am not against it. I say: Be a driftwood—whatever happens, let it happen. Don't have a choice of your own. Whatever comes your way, welcome it. Sometimes it is day, sometimes it is night; sometimes it is happiness, sometimes it is unhappiness—you be choiceless, you simply accept whatsoever is the case.

This is what I call the quality of a spiritual being. This is what I call religious consciousness. It is neither for nor against—because if you are for, you will be against; if you are against, you will be for. And when you are for something or against something you have divided existence into two. You have a choice, and choice is hell. To be choiceless is to be free of hell.

Let things be. You just go on moving, enjoying whatever becomes available. If success is there, enjoy it. If failure is there, enjoy it—because failure also brings a few enjoyments that no success can ever bring. Success brings a few joys that no failure can ever bring. And a man who has no idea of his own is capable of enjoying everything, whatever happens. If he is healthy, he enjoys health; if he is ill, he rests on the bed and enjoys illness.

Have you ever enjoyed illness? If you have not enjoyed it you are missing a lot. Just lying down on the bed doing nothing, no worry of the world and everybody caring for you, and you have suddenly become a monarch—everybody attentive, listening, loving. And you have nothing to do, not a single worry in the world. You simply rest. You listen to the birds, you listen to music, or you read a little and doze into sleep. It is beautiful! It has its own beauty. But if you have an idea that you have to be always healthy, then you will be miserable.

Misery comes because we choose. Bliss is when we don't choose.

7 of Fire: Stress

Struggling with life does not help at all. Struggling is simply destructive; there is no point in it. Effort is not needed.

All private goals are against the goal of the universe itself. All private goals are against the goal of the whole. All private goals are neurotic. One who knows the essential comes to feel, "I am not separate from the whole and there is no need to seek and search for any destiny on my own. Things are happening, the world is moving—call it existence, call it the beyond—existence is doing things. They are happening of their own accord. There is no need for me to make any struggle, any effort; there is no need for me to fight for anything. I can relax and be."

The essential man is not a doer, the accidental man is a doer. The accidental man is, of course then, in anxiety, tension, stress, anguish, continuously sitting on a volcano—it can erupt any moment, because he lives in a world of uncertainty and believes it is certain. This creates a tension in his being: he knows deep down that nothing is certain.

A rich man has everything that he can have, and yet he knows deep down that he has nothing. That's what makes a rich man even poorer than a poor man. A poor man is never so poor because still he has hopes: someday or other, destiny is going to shower blessings on him.

Someday or other he will be able to arrive, to achieve. He can hope. The rich man has arrived, his hopes are fulfilled—now, suddenly, he finds nothing is fulfilled. All hopes fulfilled and yet nothing is fulfilled. He has arrived and he has not arrived at all—it has always been a dream journey. He has not moved a single inch.

A man who is successful in the world feels the pain of being a failure as nobody else can feel it. There is a proverb that says that nothing succeeds like success. I would like to tell you that nothing fails like success. But you cannot know it unless you have succeeded. When all the riches are there that you have dreamed about, planned for, worked hard for, then sitting just amidst those riches is the beggar—deep inside empty, hollow; nothing inside, everything outside.

In fact, when everything is there outside, it becomes a contrast. It simply emphasizes your inner emptiness and nothingness. It simply emphasizes your inner beggarliness, poverty. A rich man knows poverty as no poor man can ever know it. A successful man knows what failure is. At the top of the world, suddenly you realize that you have been behaving foolishly. You may not say so, because what is the point of saying it? You may go on pretending that you are very happy— presidents and prime ministers go on pretending they are very happy. They are not. They are just saving their faces. Now, what to say? There is no point even in saying anything—they are not truthful.

In the older ages, people were truer, more authentic. Buddha was a prince. He was going to be the emperor, but he realized that there was nothing in it. He could have pretended. Mahavira was a prince; he was going to be the emperor. He realized that there was nothing in it. They simply declared their realization to the world. They simply said that riches had failed, that kingdoms were not kingdoms; that if you are really seeking the kingdom you will have to seek somewhere else, in some other direction. In *this* world there is no way to arrive.

If you have a private goal you are going to go mad. Relax! Drop out of the accidental world so you can drop into the essential world. Then one starts accepting things as they are. Then one starts loving things as they are. Then one starts cherishing things as they are. And they have always been beautiful. Once you are not fighting, not going anywhere, you can feel the music, the celestial music that is surrounding you. You can see the infinite beauty and you can feel grateful for it. It is a gift. There is no need to steal it—it is already given to you.

And once you start understanding this, the world takes on a totally new color. Even sometimes when there is pain, you are understanding. Sometimes it hurts—yes. Even then it is not all roses, it cannot be, but you start understanding it. In fact, you start seeing that thorns are there to protect the roses; that night is needed to help the day to be born; that death is needed to refresh life. Once you start understanding, you become positive. Then whatsoever happens, you can always look deeper into its meaning, its significance.

One who has attained to the essential center moves on, dancing in different situations. Sometimes it is hot, sometimes it is cold; sometimes it is joy, sometimes it is sadness—but now everything brings some message from the whole. Everything has become a messenger.

8 of Fire: Traveling

Life is a continuity, always and always. There is no final destination it is going towards. Just the pilgrimage, just the journey in itself is life, not reaching to some point, no goal.

What will you do by getting to a destination? Nobody has asked this because everybody is trying to have some destination in life. But the implications. . . .

If you really reach the destination of life, then what? Then you will look very embarrassed. Nowhere to go . . . you have reached the final destination—and in the journey you have lost everything. You had to lose everything. So standing naked at the final destination, you will look all around like an idiot: What was the point? You were hurrying so hard, and you were worrying so hard, and this is the outcome.

Rabindranath Tagore has a story. The story says in song, "I have been searching for God for centuries. Sometimes he was around the moon, but by the time I reached there he had moved to some other star. I saw him at another star, but by the time I reached there he had moved again. This went on and on, but there was great joy in the knowledge that he was there, and one day I was going to find him. How long can he hide? How long can he escape?

"And it happened that one day I reached a house where there was a sign saying that this was the house of God. I had a great sense of relief that my destiny was fulfilled. I went up the steps and I was just going to knock on the door when I had a second thought: 'What are you going to do if God comes and opens the door? What will you do next? Your whole life has been a journey, a pilgrimage, finding, searching. You are trained as a runner for millions of years, and suddenly you meet God and you don't have anything to say. What will you say?'"

Have you ever thought about it? That if you meet God by chance, neither will you have anything to say, nor will he have anything to say. You unnecessarily burned yourself out, finished. A final destination means ultimate death.

The Zen master Ikkyu is right when he says, "No final destination, nothing of any value"—everything is just to enjoy and dance and sing. But don't ask about value; don't ask what is virtue and what is good. Rejoice in everything, and go on in different pilgrimages knowing perfectly well that life is not going to end anywhere, the journey will continue, the caravan will continue. There is no place where the road ends.

Be on a pleasure trip. Let this life be a joyous journey to nowhere—from nowhere to nowhere. You come from nowhere, you go to nowhere. In the middle you exist. You come out of nothing, you disappear into nothing. In the middle is the flash of being. Enjoy it while it is there. Celebrate it. Don't destroy it in reaching somewhere; there is nowhere to reach. And, more important, there is nobody inside to reach. The traveler exists not, the traveler is a myth. The pilgrimage is true but the pilgrim is false.

9 of Fire: Exhaustion

You are not to do anything to be happy. In fact you have done too much to become unhappy. If you want to be unhappy, do too much. If you want to be happy, allow things, allow things to be. Rest, relax, and be in a let-go.

Let-go is the secret of life. When you are in a let-go, many things, millions of things start happening. They were already happening but you were never aware. You could not be aware; you were engaged somewhere else, you were occupied.

The birds go on singing. The trees go on flowering. The rivers go on flowing. The whole is continuously happening, and the whole is very psychedelic, very colorful, with infinite celebrations going on. But you are so engaged, so occupied, so closed, with not even a single window open, no cross-ventilation in you. No sunrays can penetrate you, no breeze can blow through you, you are so solid, so closed, what Leibnitz called *monads*. You are monads. Monad means something without any windows, with no opening, with every possibility of opening closed. How can you be happy? So closed, how can you participate in the mysteries all around? How can you participate in the divine?

You will have to come out. You will have to drop this enclosure, this imprisonment.

Where are you going? And you think that somewhere in the future there is some target to be achieved? Life is already here! Why wait for the future? Why postpone it for the future? Postponement is suicidal. Life is slow; that's why you cannot feel it. It is very slow, and you are insensitive; otherwise postponement is the only poison. You kill yourself by and by. You go on postponing—and you go on missing the life that is here and now.

It is very easy to be active, it is very easy to be inactive. There are people who are active, continuously active, restless, day in, day out. That's what has happened in the West: people have become superactive. They cannot sit in rest even for a single moment. Even sitting in their beautiful, comfortable chairs, they are fidgeting, they are changing their posture. They cannot be at rest. Their whole life is a turmoil; they need something to keep them occupied. They are driving themselves mad through activity.

In the East, people have become very inactive, lazy. They are dying because of their laziness. They are poor because of their laziness. They go on condemning the whole world, as if they are poor because of the world, because of other people. They are poor because they are lazy, utterly lazy. They are poor because action has completely disappeared—how can they be productive? How can they be rich? And it is not that they are poor because they have been exploited; even if you distribute all the money that the rich people in India have, the poverty will not disappear. All those rich people will become poor, that is true, but no poor persons will become rich. Poverty is there, deep down, because of inaction. And it is very easy to choose one polarity: action is male, inaction is female.

One has to do, but not become a doer. One has to do almost as if one is functioning as an instrument of God. One has to do and yet remain egoless. Act, respond, but don't become restless. When the action is complete, you have responded adequately, go into rest. Work when it is needed to work, play when it is needed to play. Rest, lie down on the beach when you have worked and played. When you are lying down on the beach under the sun, don't think of work—don't think of the office, don't think of the files. Forget all about the world.

Lying in the sun, lie in the sun. Enjoy it. This is possible only when you learn the secret of action through inaction. And then in the office, do whatsoever is needed. In the factory do whatsoever is needed, but even while you are doing, remain a witness: deep down, in deep rest, utterly centered, the periphery moving like a wheel, but the center is the center of the cyclone. Nothing is moving at the center.

This man is the perfect man: his soul is at rest, his center is absolutely tranquil, his periphery in action, in doing a thousand and one things of the world. That's why I say don't leave the world, remain in the world. Act in the world, do whatsoever is needful, and yet remain transcendental, aloof, detached, a lotus flower in the pond.

10 of Fire: Suppression

Into the unconscious you go on throwing all the rubbish that society rejects—but remember, whatsoever you throw in there becomes more and more part of you: it goes into your hands, into your bones, into your blood, into your heartbeat.

Through suppression, mind becomes split. The part that you accept becomes the conscious, and the part that you deny becomes the unconscious.

This division is not natural. The division happens because of repression. And into the unconscious you go on throwing all the rubbish that society rejects—but remember, whatever you throw in there becomes more and more part of you: it goes into your hands, into your bones, into your blood, into your heartbeat.

Now psychologists say that almost eighty percent of diseases are caused by repressed emotions: so many heart failures means so much anger has been repressed in the heart, so much hatred that the heart is poisoned.

Why? Why does man suppress so much and become unhealthy? Because the society teaches you to control, not to transform, and the way of transformation is totally different. For one thing, it is not the way of control at all; it is just the opposite.

In controlling you repress. In transformation you express. But there is no need to express on somebody else because the "somebody else" is just irrelevant. Next time you feel angry, go and run around the house seven times and then sit under a tree and watch: Where has the anger gone? You have not repressed it, you have not controlled it, you have not thrown it on somebody else—because if you throw it on somebody else, a chain is created because the other is as foolish as you, as unconscious as you. If you throw it on another, and if the other is an enlightened person, there will be no trouble; he will help you to throw and release it and go through a catharsis. But the other is as ignorant as you are—if you throw anger on him he will react. He will throw more anger on you, he is as repressed as you are. Then a chain is created: you throw anger on the other, the other throws anger on you, and you become enemies.

Don't throw it on anybody. It is the same as when you feel like vomiting: you don't go and vomit on somebody. Something needs to be vomited, you go to the bathroom and vomit! It cleanses the whole body—if you suppress the vomit, it will be dangerous. And when you have vomited you will feel fresh, you will feel better, unburdened, unloaded, healthier. Something was wrong in the food that you took and the body rejected it. Don't go on forcing it inside.

Anger is just a mental vomit. Something is wrong that you have taken in and your whole psychic being wants to throw it out. There is no need to throw it out on somebody else. But because people throw it on others, society tells them to control it.

There is no need to throw anger on anybody. You can go to your bathroom, you can go on a long walk—it means that something is inside that needs some activity so that it can be released. Just do a little jogging and you will feel it is released, or take a pillow and beat the pillow, fight with the pillow, and bite the pillow until your hands and teeth are relaxed. With a five-minute catharsis you will feel unburdened. And once you know this you will never throw it on anybody, because that is absolutely foolish.

The first thing in transformation, then, is to express anger—but not on anybody, because if you express it on somebody you cannot express it totally. You might like to kill the person, but it is not possible; you might want to bite somebody, but it is not possible. But that can be done to a pillow. A pillow means "already enlightened!" The pillow is enlightened, a buddha; it will not react, and it will not go to any court. The pillow will not feel any enmity toward you, it will not do anything. The pillow will be happy, it will laugh at you!

The second thing to remember: Be aware. In controlling, no awareness is needed; you simply do it mechanically, like a robot. The anger comes and there is a mechanism—suddenly your whole being becomes narrow and closed. If you are watchful, control may not be so easy.

Society never teaches you to be watchful, because when somebody is watchful he is wide open. That is part of awareness—one is open. And if you want to suppress something and you are open, it is contradictory; it may come out. The society teaches you how to close yourself in, how to cave yourself in—don't allow even a small window for anything to go out.

But remember: When nothing goes out, nothing comes in either. When the anger cannot go out, you are closed. If you touch a beautiful rock, nothing goes in. You look at a flower, nothing goes in; your eyes are dead and closed. You kiss a person—nothing goes in, because you are closed. You live an insensitive life.

Sensitivity grows with awareness. Through control you become dull and dead—that is part of the mechanism of control. If you are dull and dead then nothing will affect you, as if the body has become a citadel, defended. Nothing will affect you, neither insult nor love.

But this control is at a very great cost, an unnecessary cost; then it becomes the whole effort in life: how to control yourself—and then die! The whole effort of control takes all your energy, and then you simply die. And life becomes a dull and dead thing; you somehow carry it.

Awareness is needed, not condemnation—and through awareness, transformation happens spontaneously.

THE SUIT OF WATER
(CUPS)

Feelings—The Heart—Emotion

Knowing is cerebral, feeling is total. When you feel, you don't feel only from the head, you don't feel only from your heart, you don't feel only from your guts; you feel from every fiber of your being. Feeling is total, feeling is orgasmic, feeling is organic.

Feelings

In a moment of feeling, you function as a totality. When you think, you function only as the head. When you are sentimental, you function only as the heart. Remember, sentimentality is not feeling, emotionalism is not feeling. Thinking, you are a head—just a part pretending to be the whole. Of course it is false. This perspective is false. Emotional, sentimental, you are the heart—again another part pretending to be the whole, another servant pretending to be the master. Again it is false.

Feeling is of the total—of the body, of the mind, of the soul. Feeling knows no divisions; feeling is indivisible. When you feel, you function as a totality. When you function as a totality you function in tune with the totality. Let me repeat it: when you function as a totality you function in tune with the totality. When you function as a part you have fallen apart; you are no longer in tune with the total. When you are no longer in tune with the total, whatsoever you think you know is false, illusory. When you are in tune with the total, you know that you don't know anything. But even this "not knowing" is a knowing—it is a feeling, it is a love affair with the whole.

The Heart

The heart knows no negative language. The heart never asks, "What is beauty?" It enjoys it, and in enjoying it, it knows what beauty is. It cannot define it, it cannot explain itself, because the experience is such that it is inexplicable, inexpressible. Language is not adequate; no symbols help. The heart knows what love is—but don't ask. The mind knows only questions and the heart knows only answers. The mind goes on asking but it cannot answer.

Hence philosophy has no answers . . . questions and questions and questions. Each question becomes, slowly, a thousand and one questions. The heart has no questions—it is one of the mysteries of life—it has all the answers. But the mind will not listen to the heart; there is no communication between the two, no communication, because the heart knows only the language of silence. No other language is known by the heart, no other language is understood by the heart. And the mind knows nothing of silence. The mind is all noise, a tale told by an idiot, full of sound and fury noise, signifying nothing.

The heart knows what significance is. The heart knows the glory of life, the tremendous joy of sheer existence. The heart is capable of celebrating, but it never asks. Hence the mind thinks the heart is blind. The mind is full of doubts, the heart is full of trust; they are polar opposites.

But remember: the positive is joined with the negative, two sides of the same phenomenon.

I am not here to teach you the ways of the heart. Yes, I use them, but only as a device. To bring you out of your mind, I use the heart as a vehicle; to take you to the other shore I use the heart as a boat. Once you have reached the other shore, the boat has to be left behind; you are not expected to carry the boat on your head.

The goal is to go beyond duality. The goal is to go beyond no and yes both, because your yes can have meaning only in the context of no; it cannot be free of the no. If it is free of the no, what meaning will it have? Your yes can exist only with the no, remember; and your no can also exist only with the yes. They are polar opposites, but they help each other in a subtle way. There is a conspiracy! They are holding hands, they are supporting each other because they cannot exist separately. Yes has meaning only because of the no; no has meaning only because of the yes. And you have to go beyond this conspiracy, you have to go beyond this duality.

Emotions

Will it ever be possible for the head and heart to be married, or are they going to remain forever divorced? It all depends on you, because both are mechanisms. You are neither the head nor the heart. You can move through the head, you can move through the heart. Of course you will reach different places because the directions of the head and the heart are diametrically opposite.

The head will go round and round thinking, brooding, philosophizing; it knows only words, logic, argument. But it is very infertile; you cannot get anything out of the head as far as truth is concerned, because truth needs no logic, no argument, no philosophical research. Truth is so simple; the head makes it so complex. Down the centuries philosophers have been seeking and searching for the truth through the head. None of them has found anything, but they have created great systems of thought. I have looked into all those systems: they never come to any conclusion.

The heart is also a mechanism—different from the head. You can call the head the logical instrument; you can call the heart the emotional instrument. Out of the head all the philosophies, all the theologies are created; out of the heart comes all kinds of devotion, prayer, sentimentality. But the heart also goes round and round in emotions.

The word *emotion* is good. Watch . . . it consists of motion, movement. So the heart moves, but the heart is blind. It moves fast, quick, because there is no reason to wait. It does not have to think, so it jumps into anything. But truth is not to be found by any emotionality. Emotion is as much a barrier as logic.

The logic is the male in you, and the heart is the female in you. But truth has nothing to do with male and female. Truth is your consciousness. You can watch the head thinking, you can watch the heart throbbing with emotion. They can be in a certain relationship. . . .

Ordinarily, the society has arranged that the head should be the master and the heart should be the servant, because society is the creation of man's mind, psychology, and the heart is feminine. Just as man has kept the woman a slave, the head has kept the heart a slave.

We can reverse the situation: the heart can become the master and the head can become the servant. If we have to choose between the two, if we are forced to choose between the two, then it is better that the heart becomes the master and the head becomes the servant.

There are things that the heart is incapable of. Exactly the same is true about the head. The head cannot love, it cannot feel, it is insensitive. The heart cannot be rational, reasonable. For the whole past they have been in conflict. That conflict only represents the conflict and struggle between men and women.

If a man is talking to his wife, he knows it is impossible to talk, it is impossible to argue, it is impossible to come to a fair decision because the woman functions through the heart. She jumps from one thing to another without bothering whether there is any relationship between the two. She cannot argue, but she can cry. She cannot be rational, but she can scream. She cannot be cooperative in coming to a conclusion. The heart cannot understand the language of the head.

The difference is not much as far as physiology is concerned; the heart and the head are just a few inches apart from each other. But as far as their existential qualities are concerned, they are poles apart.

My way has been described as that of the heart, but it is not true. The heart will give you all kinds of imaginings, hallucinations, illusions, sweet dreams—but it cannot give you the truth. The truth is behind both; it is in your consciousness, which is neither head nor heart. Just because the consciousness is separate from both, it can use both in harmony. The head is dangerous in certain fields, because it has eyes but it has no legs—it is crippled.

The heart can function in certain dimensions. It has no eyes but it has legs; it is blind but it can move tremendously, with great speed— of course, not knowing where it is going. It is not just a coincidence that in all the languages of the world love is called blind. It is not love that is blind, it is the heart that has no eyes.

As your meditation becomes deeper, as your identification with the head and the heart starts falling, you find yourself becoming a triangle. And your reality is in the third force in you: the consciousness. Consciousness can manage very easily, because the heart and the head both belong to it.

A conscious person uses the head as a servant, and the heart as the master. But right now, and for centuries, just the opposite has been happening: the servant has become the master. And the master is so polite, such a gentleman, that he has not fought back, he has accepted the slavery voluntarily. The madness on the earth is the result.

We have to change the very alchemy of humanity. We have to rearrange the whole inside of man. And the most basic revolution in humanity will come when the heart decides the values. It cannot decide for war, it cannot go for nuclear weapons; it cannot be death-oriented. The heart is life's juice. Once the head is in the service of the heart, it has to do what the heart decides. And the head is immensely capable of doing anything, just right guidance is needed; otherwise, it is going to go berserk, it is going to be mad. For the head there are no values. For the head there is no meaning in anything. For the head there is no love, no beauty, no grace—only reasoning.

But this miracle is possible only by disidentifying yourself from both. Watch the thoughts, because in your watching them, they disappear. Then watch your emotions, sentimentalities; by your watching, they also disappear. Then your heart is as innocent as that of a child, and your head is as great a genius as Albert Einstein, Bertrand Russell, Aristotle.

King of Water: Healing

Be aware of your wound. Don't help it to grow, let it be healed; and it will be healed only when you move to the roots. Go to the roots. Be with the whole.

Everybody is born to remain healthy and happy. Everybody is seeking health and happiness, but somewhere something is missing and everybody becomes miserable. Misery should be an exception; it has become the rule. Happiness should be the rule; it has become an exception. I would like a world where buddhas are born, but nobody remembers them because they are the rule. Now Buddha is remembered, Christ is remembered, Lao Tzu is remembered, because they are exceptions. Otherwise, who would bother about them? If there were a buddha in every house, and if there were buddhas all over the marketplace and you could meet Lao Tzu anywhere, who would bother? Then that would be the simple rule. It should be so.

Lao Tzu says that when the world was really moral there was no possibility of becoming a saint. When the world was really religious there was no need for religions. People were simply religious; religions were not needed. When there was order, discipline—a *natural* order and discipline. The words *order* and *discipline* didn't exist. The idea of order comes in only when there is disorder. People start talking about discipline where there is no discipline, and people talk about healing when there is illness. People talk about love when love is missing. But basically, therapy is a function of love.

Never look at a patient as a patient. Look at him as if he has come to learn something—a disciple. Help him, but not as an expert; help him like a human being, and there will be much healing. There will be less therapy and much healing. Otherwise, therapy continues for years and years on end, and the result is almost nil. Or, sometimes the result is even harmful.

The word *meditation* and the word *medicine* come from the same root. Medicine means that which heals the physical and meditation means that which heals the spiritual. Both are healing powers.

Another thing to be remembered: the word *healing* and the word *whole* also come from the same root. To be healed simply means to be whole, not missing anything. Another connotation of the word—the word *holy*—also comes from the same root. Healing, whole, and holy are not different in their root.

Meditation heals, makes you whole; and to be whole is to be holy. Holiness has nothing to do with belonging to any religion, belonging to any church. It simply means that inside you, you are entire, complete; nothing is missing, you are fulfilled. You are what existence wanted you to be. You have realized your potential.

Queen of Water: Receptivity

One has to become feminine. One has to become receptive rather than being aggressive. One has to learn the art of relaxation rather than learning the strategies of how to conquer the world.

Inactivity is negative, receptivity is positive. They look very similar. You will need very penetrating eyes to see the difference between the inactive and the receptive. The receptive is a welcome, it is an awaiting, it has a prayer in it. Receptivity is a host, receptivity is a womb. Inactivity is simply dullness, death, hopelessness. There is nothing to wait for, nothing to expect, nothing is ever going to happen. It is falling into lethargy; it is falling into a kind of indifference. And indifference and lethargy are poisons.

But the same thing that becomes indifference can become detachment, and then it has a totally different flavor. Indifference looks like detachment, but it is not; indifference is simply no interest. Detachment is not absence of interest—detachment is absolute interest, tremendous interest, but still with the capacity of non-clinging. Enjoy the moment while it is there and when the moment starts disappearing, as everything is bound to disappear, let it go. That is detachment.

Lethargy is a negative state. One is like a lump of mud just lying there—no possibility of growth, no exuberance, no flowering. But the same energy can become a pool, a great pool of energy—not going anywhere, not doing anything, but the energy accumulating and accumulating and accumulating.

And scientists say that at a certain point the quantitative change becomes a qualitative change. At a hundred degrees heat the water evaporates. At ninety-nine degrees it has not evaporated yet; at ninety-nine point nine degrees it has still not evaporated. But just point one degree more, and the water will take a quantum leap.

Positive feminineness is not like lethargy, it is like a tremendous pool of energy. And as the energy gathers and accumulates, it goes through many qualitative changes.

Knight of Water: Trust

Trust is yes. Knowing that this existence is our mother, that nature is our source and it can't be against us, it can't be inimical to us. Seeing this, understanding this, trust arises.

Remember: one has to take the jump, even when there is doubt. If you wait to let doubt subside first, then the time will never come for you to take the jump because doubt is a self-creating process. One doubt creates another; another doubt creates another. And the same happens with trust—one trust creates another, another trust . . . then a chain is created. When you start, there is always a wavering. Nobody can start with a total heart because then there would be no need. One has to start with doubt, but don't pay much attention to the doubt—pay much attention to trust. Then the energy moves towards trust, and the trust creates a chain. By and by, the energy of doubt is absorbed by the energy of trust.

You have always been here, but you have missed many times. Why? The reason is always the same—you cannot trust. You go on finding arguments against taking a jump; and there are infinite possibilities to go on finding arguments again and again and again. Because once you feed doubt it becomes a cancerous growth—then it perpetuates itself, there is no need to help it. It is a cancerous growth, it goes on and on, and it grows. The same thing happens with trust.

So remember that it is not a question of "When there is no doubt then I will trust." It is impossible, that time will never come. You have to trust while doubt is there.

And look at the beauty of it! If you can trust while doubt is there—and this is how human mind is, frail, weak, divided; you have to trust while doubt is there—if you can trust while doubt is there, it means that you pay more attention to trust and less attention to doubt. You are indifferent to doubt, your whole attention is on trust. Then a day comes when the doubt has disappeared, because if you don't give attention you don't give food—attention is food. If you don't give attention the doubt cannot persist in its chain.

Page of Water: Understanding

In your very understanding you are free.

You can understand only as much as you have experienced; understanding never goes beyond your experience. Words you can accumulate, you can become scholars, great scholars. And you will be in a new kind of illusion, the illusion that information creates. The more information you have, the more you start feeling you know.

Information is thought to be synonymous with knowing—it is not. Knowing is a totally different affair. Knowing is experiencing; information only accumulates in the memory system. A computer can do it, there is nothing special about it; there is nothing especially human about it.

Two large rats walked into a movie house one day and went straight to the projection room. Once inside they ate the entire reel of film. After eating, one rat looked at the other and asked, "Did you like the movie?"

To which the other replied, "No, I liked the book better."

These are the scholars—the rats! They go on eating words, they go on accumulating words. They can have mountains of words and they become very articulate about words. They can deceive others; that is not so bad because they can deceive only people who are already deceived; you cannot do much more harm to them. But by deceiving others, slowly they become deceived themselves, and that is the greatest problem.

When the head understands, then it asks, "How? Yes it *is* right; now, how can it be done?" Remember this difference: in the head, knowledge and action are two different things; in the heart, knowledge *is* action.

Socrates says that knowledge is virtue—and he has not been understood down the ages. Not even his own disciples, Plato and Aristotle, have understood him rightly. When he says knowledge is virtue, he means there is a way of listening and understanding where the moment you understand a thing, you can't do otherwise. When you see that this is the door, then you cannot try to get out through the wall. You will go out through the door. Seeing means acting, seeing brings action.

But I tell you, "This is the door, so whenever you want to get out, please go through this door, because you have hurt your head enough by trying to get out through the wall." And you say, "Yes, sir, I understand perfectly well, but how do I get out through the door?" Your question will show that the heart has not listened, only the head. The head always asks "How?"

The head always asks questions that seem to be very pertinent on the surface but are absolutely ridiculous. The heart never asks—it listens and acts. Listening and action are one in the heart. Love knows, and acts accordingly. It never asks "How?" The heart has an intelligence of its own. The head is intellectual, the heart is intelligence.

Just a little bit of understanding can bring a tremendous revolution in your life. All seeds are small—the trees may grow high, almost touching the stars, but the seeds are very small. This is just a seed that has fallen into your heart; now allow it to grow. Give nourishment to it, support it, remove all hindrances in its path, and a small seed, which seems to be nothing special in this moment, may bring thousands of flowers.

Ace of Water: Going with the Flow

GOING WITH THE FLOW

Trust means you are not fighting; surrender means you don't think of life as the enemy but as the friend. Once you trust the river, suddenly you start enjoying.

You swim in water—you go to the river and swim. What do you do? You trust the water. A good swimmer trusts so much that he almost becomes one with the river. He is not fighting, he does not grab the water, he is not stiff and tense.

If you are stiff and tense you will be drowned; if you are relaxed, the river takes care. That's why whenever somebody dies, the dead body floats on the water. This is a miracle, amazing! The alive person died and was drowned by the river, and the dead person simply floats on the surface. What has happened? The dead person knows some secret about the river that the alive person did not know. The alive person was fighting. The river was the enemy, he was afraid, he could not trust. But the dead person, not being there, how can he fight? The dead person is totally relaxed with no tension—suddenly the body surfaces. The river takes care. No river can drown a dead person.

Trust means you are not fighting; surrender means you don't think of life as the enemy but as the friend. Once you trust the river, suddenly you start enjoying. Tremendous delight arises: splashing, swimming or just floating, or diving deep. But you are not separate from the river; you merge, you become one.

Surrender means to live the same way in life as a good swimmer swims in the river. Life is a river. Either you can fight or you can float; either you can push the river and try to go against the current, or you can float with the river and go wherever the river leads you.

The water is non-aggressive, it never fights—it makes its way without fighting. It is from water that the Chinese and Japanese learned the secret art of judo or jujitsu. Winning without fighting, conquering through surrendering—*wei-wu-wei*.

Learn one thing from the water: it comes across great stone walls, granite walls; it does not fight. It goes on flowing silently. If a stone is too big, it finds another way; it bypasses it. But slowly the stone is dissolved into the water, becomes sand. Ask the sands of the oceans from where they have come. They have come from the mountains. They will tell you a great secret: "Water wins finally. And we were hard, and we thought, 'How can the water win?' So we were very complacent. We could not believe that this poor water, so soft, harmless, unhurting, non-violent . . . how could it destroy us? But it destroyed us."

That is the beauty of the feminine energy. Don't be like a rock! Be like water—soft, feminine.

2 of Water: Friendliness

Rather than creating friendship, create friendliness.

Let it become a quality of your being, a climate that surrounds you, so you are friendly with whomsoever you come in contact.

Do you know what friendship is? It is the highest form of love. In love, some lust is bound to be there; in friendship, all lust disappears. In friendship nothing gross remains; it becomes absolutely subtle.

It is not a question of using the other, it is not even a question of needing the other; it is a question of sharing. You have too much and you would like to share. And whoever is ready to share your joy with you, your dance, your song, you will be grateful to them, you will feel obliged. Not that the other is obliged to you. Not that he should feel thankful to you because you have given so much to him. A friend never thinks in that way. A friend always feels grateful to those people who allow him to love them, to give them whatever he has.

Love is greed. You will be surprised to know that the English word *love* comes from a Sanskrit word *lobh*; *lobh* means greed. How *lobh* became *love* is strange. In Sanskrit it is greed; the original root means greed. And love as we know it is really nothing but greed masquerading as love—it is hidden greed.

Making friendships with the idea of using people is taking a wrong step from the very beginning. Friendship has to be a sharing. If you have something, share it—and whosoever is ready to share with you is a friend. It is not a question of need. It is not a question that when you are in danger the friend has to come to your aid. That is irrelevant—he may come, he may not come, but if he does not come you don't have any complaint. If he comes you are grateful but if he does not come, it's perfectly okay. It is his decision to come or not to come. You don't want to manipulate him; you don't want to make him feel guilty. You will not have any grudge. You will not say, "When I was in need you didn't turn up—what kind of friend are you?"

Friendship is not something of the marketplace. Friendship is one of those rare things that belong to the temple and not to the shop. But if you are not aware of that kind of friendship, you will have to learn it.

Friendship is a great art.

And friendship need not be addressed to anyone in particular; that is also a rotten idea, that you have to be friends with a certain person. Just be friendly. Rather than creating friendship, create friendliness. Let it become a quality of your being, a climate that surrounds you, so you are friendly with whomever you come in contact.

This whole existence has to be befriended! And if you can befriend existence, existence will befriend you a thousandfold. It returns to you in the same coin but multiplied. It echoes you. If you throw stones at existence you will be getting back many more stones. If you throw flowers, flowers will be coming back.

Life is a mirror, it reflects your face. Be friendly, and all of life will reflect friendliness.

You can be friendly to many people and there is no question of jealousy. It does not matter that you are friendly to five persons or ten persons or ten thousand persons; nobody will feel deprived because you love so many people and his share is going to be less and less. On the contrary, as you are able to love more people, your quality of love becomes mountainous. So whomever you love gets more love if your love is shared with many people. It dies if it is narrowed. It becomes livelier if it is spread over a vast area—the bigger the area, the deeper are its roots.

Consciousness gives everything a transformation. Your love is no longer addressed to anybody in particular. It does not mean that you stop loving. It simply means you *become* love, you *are* love, your very being is love. Your breathing is love, your heartbeats are love. Awake you are love, asleep you are love.

And the same is true about everything else—your understanding, your intelligence, everything goes through the same change. You become the center of the whole existence, the center of the cyclone, and everything radiates from you and reaches anybody who is able to receive it.

It is not a question of loving someone for certain reasons; it is love simply out of abundance—you have so much that you have to share it, you have to radiate it. And whoever receives it, you are grateful to the person.

3 of Water: Celebration

Celebration is a thankfulness; it is prayer out of gratitude.

It is recognition of the gift that has been given to us . . .

It is such an immense gift to be alive, but people are very ungrateful; they have forgotten how to give thanks. They never feel the awe of existence, they never feel so grateful that they need to bow down to the earth. They are utterly stonelike, unfeeling, unseeing. And because of these people—and they are the majority—the whole of life has become ugly. It is because of these people that life has lost its joys, celebrations.

Remember: animals can play but only man can celebrate. It is man's privilege and prerogative; no other animal can celebrate. Yes, they can play, but play is one thing and celebration is totally another. Celebration is a thankfulness; it is prayer that comes out of gratitude. It is recognition of the gift that has been given to us . . . it is understanding. It is overflowing love for the existence that has done so much for us. Just to be alive is so festive. Even for a single moment to feel the rain and to see the sun and to be on the beach, even for a single moment to see the stars, is enough for a person to become religious.

There is no need to postpone celebration. Immediately, right this moment, you can celebrate. Nothing else is needed. To celebrate, life is needed—and life you have. To celebrate, being is needed—and being you have. To celebrate, trees and birds and stars are needed, and they are there. What else do you need? If you are crowned and caged in a golden palace, then will you celebrate? In fact, then it will become more impossible. Have you ever seen an emperor laughing and dancing and singing in the street? No, he is caged, imprisoned by manners, etiquette . . .

Somewhere, Bertrand Russell has written that when for the first time he visited a primitive community of aboriginals living deep in some hills, he felt jealous, very jealous. He felt that the way they danced . . . it was as if everybody were an emperor. They had no crowns, but they had made crowns with leaves and with flowers. Every woman was a queen. They didn't have Kohinoors, but whatsoever they had was so much, it was enough. They danced the whole night and then they fell asleep, there on the dancing ground. By the morning they were again back to work. They worked the whole day, and again by the evening they were ready to celebrate, to dance. Russell says, "That day, I felt really jealous. I cannot do this."

Something has gone wrong. Something is frustrated within you; you cannot dance, you cannot sing, something is withheld. You live a crippled life. It was never meant for you to be crippled, but you live a crippled life, you live a paralyzed life. And you go on thinking that being ordinary, how can you celebrate? There is nothing special in you.

But who told you that to celebrate something special is needed? In fact, the more you are after the special, the more and more it will become difficult for you to dance.

Be ordinary. Nothing is wrong with ordinariness, because in your very ordinariness you are extraordinary. Don't bother about what conditions will decide when you can celebrate. If you bother about fulfilling certain conditions, do you think that then you will celebrate? You will never celebrate, you will die a beggar. Why not right now? What are you lacking?

This is my observation: if you can start right now, suddenly the energy is flowing. And the more you dance, the more it is flowing, the more capable you become. The ego needs conditions to be fulfilled, not life. Birds can sing and dance, ordinary birds. Have you ever seen any extraordinary birds singing and dancing? Do they ask that they first have to be a Ravi Shankar or a Yehudi Menuhin? Do they ask that first they have to be great singers and go to colleges of music to learn, and then they will sing? They simply dance and simply sing; no training is needed.

Man is born with the capacity to celebrate. When even birds can celebrate, why not you? But you create unnecessary barriers, you create a hurdle race. There are no barriers. You put them there and then you say, "Unless we cross them and jump over them, how can we dance?" You stand divided against yourself, you are an enemy to yourself.

All the preachers in the world go on saying that you are ordinary, so how can you dare to celebrate? You have to wait. First be a Buddha, first be a Jesus, a Mohammed, and then you can. But just the opposite is the case. If you can dance, you are already the Buddha; if you can celebrate, you are already a Mohammed; if you can be blissful, you are already a Jesus. The contrary is not true; the contrary is a false logic. It says first be a Buddha, then you can celebrate. But how will you be a Buddha without celebrating?

Celebrate, forget all buddhas. In your very celebration you will find that you have yourself become a buddha. And when I say celebrate, I mean become more and more sensitive to everything. In life, dance should not be just a part. The whole of life should become a dance; it should be a dance. You can go for a walk and dance . . .

Allow life to enter into you. Become more open and vulnerable, feel more, sense more. Small things filled with such wonders are lying all around. Watch a small child; leave him in the garden and just watch. That should be your way also; so wonderful, wonder-filled. Running to catch this butterfly, running to catch that flower, playing with mud, rolling in the sand. From everywhere the divine is touching the child.

If you can live in wonder you will be capable of celebration. Don't live in knowledge, live in wonder. You don't know anything. Life is surprising; everywhere it is a continuous surprise. Live it as a surprise, an unpredictable phenomenon; every moment is new. Just try, give it a try! You will not lose anything if you give it a try, and you may gain everything.

4 of Water: Turning In

Meditation is the whole art of transforming the gestalt. The consciousness that goes outward starts turning in.

And then one becomes aware of millions of gifts; then small things, very small and ordinary things have tremendous significance.

Meditation means a one-hundred-and-eighty-degree turn. Ordinarily we are focused on the outside; in meditation we change the focus. We are focused on ourselves. Meditation means the experience of your own interiority; it is an inward journey.

And once you have tasted even a single drop of the nectar, then the misery, the anguish, the whole "problematic" life dissolves. Now you know the right direction to go; now you know the right door at which to knock. . . .

Jesus says, "Knock and the door shall be opened unto you." But the question is on what door, where to knock? Knocking on just any door is not going to help. Unless you start knocking on the inner door nothing is going to happen. Jesus says, "Ask and it shall be given." But whom to ask? People have been asking the sky, the heavens, God the Father, somewhere above there in the clouds. For centuries they have been asking and nothing has been answered. One has to ask one's own inner core.

Jesus says, "Seek and ye shall find." But where to seek? People have been seeking in every sacred place; they are going to Jerusalem or to Mecca or to Kashi or to Tibet. That is not going to help. Wherever you go, you are wasting your time. One has to go within. The kingdom of God is *within* you.

Meditation is the whole art of transforming the gestalt. The consciousness that goes outward starts turning in. And then one becomes aware of millions of gifts; then small things, very small and ordinary things, have tremendous significance. Just a dewdrop slipping from the lotus leaf into the lake is enough to fill one with wonder and awe. It is poetry, pure poetry! It is music, it is dance, it is a finger pointing to the moon.

Turning in is not a turning at all. Going in is not a going at all. Turning inward simply means that you have been running after this desire and that, and you have been running and running and you have been coming again and again to frustration that each desire brings misery, that there is no fulfillment through desire. . . . That you never reach anywhere, that contentment is impossible. Seeing this truth, that running after desires takes you nowhere, you stop. Not that you make any effort to stop! If you make any effort to stop, it is again running, in a subtle way. You are still desiring—maybe now it is desirelessness that you desire.

If you are making an effort to go in, you are still going out. Any effort can only take you out, outwards. All journeys are outward journeys, there is no inward journey. How can you journey inward? You are already there, there is no point in going. When going stops, journeying disappears. When desiring is no longer clouding your mind, you *are* in. This is called turning in. But it is not a turning at all, it is simply not going out.

But in language it is always a problem to express these things.

Once the energy is not moving anywhere. . . . Remember, I repeat again, turning in is not moving in. When the energy is not moving at all, when there is no movement, when everything is still, when all has stopped—because seeing the futility of desire you cannot move anywhere, there is nowhere to go—stillness descends. The world stops. That's what is meant by turning in. Suddenly you are in. You have always been there, now you are awake. The night is over, the morning has come, you are awake. This is what is meant by buddhahood— to become aware, awake, of that which is already the case.

Remember the Zen master Hakuin's saying: From the very beginning all beings are buddhas. From the very beginning to the very end—in the beginning, in the middle, in the end, all are buddhas. Not for a single moment have you been anybody else.

5 of Water: Clinging to the Past

A person who lives in the present—neither bothering about the past nor bothering about the future—is fresh, young; he is neither a child nor an old man.

And one can remain young to the very last breath.

One thing that has to be remembered is that the past is no more, and clinging to the past is clinging to the dead. It is very dangerous, because it hampers and hinders your life in the present, and for the future. One should always go on freeing oneself of the dead past. That is one of the fundamentals of life, to go on renewing yourself every moment, to die to the past and be born anew. That which is gone is gone—don't even look back. Looking back is not a good sign.

Small children never look back; they always look ahead. They don't have anything in the past to look back on—there is no past, they have only the future. Old men never look at the future, because in the future there is only death, and they want to avoid it, they don't want to talk about it. They always look back. They decorate their memories; they make them look very beautiful. All that they have is a collection of memories, and they go on improving on those memories. When they were actually living them, they did not enjoy them, but now the future is darkness; one needs some consolation. They can find consolation only in the past.

A person who lives in the present—neither bothering about the past nor bothering about the future—is fresh, young. He is neither a child nor an old man. And one can remain young to the very last breath. The body may be old but the consciousness remains fresh, just like a fresh breeze, cool, fragrant in the early morning sun.

The whole problem is that we are caught up with our past. It is holding us back, it does not allow us to go against it. And if you don't go against it, your whole life will be simply boredom, because you will be repeating and repeating the same past, the same routine.

Time is still, just as space is still. It neither goes anywhere nor comes from anywhere. It is just our language that goes on saying that time is passing. In fact, *we* are passing; time stands still. Time is still; only the mind is moving.

These tenses—past, present, and future—are not the tenses of time; they are tenses of the mind. That which is no longer in front of the mind becomes the past. That which is in front of the mind is the present. And that which is going to be in front of the mind is the future.

Past is that which is no longer in front of you. Future is that which is not yet in front of you. And present is that which is in front of you and is slipping out of your sight. Soon it will be past.

What is gone is gone!

And don't cling to the present, because that is also going and soon it will be past. Don't cling to the future—hopes, imaginations, plans for tomorrow—because tomorrow will become today, will become yesterday. Everything is going to become yesterday.

Everything is going to go out of your hands. Clinging will simply create misery.

You will have to let go. You cannot manage to prevent the process of things moving out of your sight, so it is better just to watch, just to witness and let things be wherever they want—in the past, in the present, in the future. Don't you be disturbed, because everything is going to fall into the past.

Only one thing is going to remain with you: that is your witnessing, that is your watchfulness. This watchfulness is meditation.

Mind is a clinger—it clings, it hoards, it possesses. In the name of memory it collects all the past. In the name of planning for the future it clings to hopes, desires, ambitions—and it suffers. Mind is continuously in tension, is continuously in anguish—always in a turmoil.

Buddha has said: If you can just remain silent and a witness, every misery, every worry, every tension will disappear. And there will be a silence and a clarity that you had never even thought about.

6 of Water: The Dream

Deep down there are dreams and dreams and dreams. An undercurrent of dreaming goes on— and that undercurrent goes on corrupting our vision.

Only when the dreaming mind has stopped is there truth. Why? Because the dreaming mind continuously projects and distorts that which is. If you look at a thing with desire, you never look at the thing as it is. Your desire starts playing games with you.

A woman passes by, a beautiful woman, or a man passes by, a handsome man—suddenly there is desire: to possess her, to possess him. Then you cannot see the reality. Then your very desire creates a dream around the object. Then you start seeing the way you would like to see. Then you start projecting—the other becomes a screen and your deepest desires are projected. You start coloring the object; then you don't see that which is. You start seeing visions, you start moving into fantasy.

Of course, this fantasy is bound to be shattered. When the reality erupts, your dreaming mind will be shattered. It happens many times. You fall in love with a woman and then, one day, suddenly, the dream has disappeared. The woman does not look so beautiful as she used to look. You cannot believe how you were deceived into being with her. You start finding faults with the woman. You start finding rationalizations—as if she tricked you into it, as if she deceived you, as if she pretended to be beautiful when in fact she was not.

Nobody is cheating you—nobody *can* cheat you except your own desiring and dreaming mind. You created the illusion. You never saw the reality of the woman. Sooner or later reality will win over.

That's how all love affairs are always on the rocks. And lovers become afraid, by and by, to see the reality—they avoid it. The wife avoids the husband, the husband avoids the wife. They don't look directly at each other. They are afraid. They are already aware that the dream has disappeared. Now, don't rock the boat. Now, avoid each other.

Husbands stop seeing things that they used to see in their wives. Wives stop seeing things in their husbands that they used to see. What happens? The reality remains the same, only against the reality the dream cannot win forever. Sooner or later the dream is shattered. And that happens in all directions.

Man continuously dreams about power, prestige, respectability. And whenever he gets it, there is frustration. The happiest people are those who never attain to their desires. The unhappiest people are those who have succeeded in attaining their desires—then there is frustration.

The nature of desire is dreaming, and you can dream only when things are not there. You can dream about the neighbor's wife—how can you dream about your own wife? Have you ever dreamt about your own wife? It never happens. You can dream about somebody else's wife. *He* may be dreaming about your wife. . . .

Whatever is far away looks beautiful. Come closer and things start changing. Reality is shattering.

To be aware means not to dream, to be aware means to drop this unconscious sleep in which we live ordinarily. We are somnambulists, sleepwalkers. We go on living, but our living is superficial. Deep down there are dreams and dreams and dreams. An undercurrent of dreaming goes on—and that undercurrent goes on corrupting our vision. That undercurrent of dreaming goes on making our eyes cloudy. That undercurrent of dreams goes on making our heads muddled.

A person who lives in a sort of sleep can never be intelligent—and awareness is the purest flame of intelligence. A person who lives in sleep becomes more and more stupid. If you live in stupor, you will become stupid, you will become dull.

This dullness has to be destroyed. And it can be destroyed only by becoming more aware.

Start contemplating in this way: if you are walking on the street, contemplate that people passing by are all dreams. The shops and the shop-keepers and the customers and the people coming and going, all are dreams. The houses, the buses, the train, the airplane, all are dreams.

You will be immediately surprised by something of tremendous import happening within you. The moment you think, "All are dreams," suddenly, like a flash, one thing comes into your vision: "I am a dream too." Because if the seen is a dream, then who is this "I"? If the object is a dream, then the subject is also a dream. If the object is false, how can the subject be the truth? Impossible.

If you watch everything as a dream, suddenly you will find something slipping out of your being: the idea of the ego. This is the only way to drop the ego, and the simplest. Just try it—meditate this way.

Meditating this way again and again, one day the miracle happens: you look in, and the ego is not found there.

The ego is a by-product, a by-product of the illusion that whatsoever you are seeing is true. If you think that objects are true, then the ego can exist; it is a by-product. If you think that objects are dreams, the ego disappears. And if you think continuously that all is a dream, then one day, in a dream in the night, you will be surprised: suddenly in the dream you will remember that this is a dream too! And immediately, as the remembrance happens, the dream will disappear. And for the first time you will experience yourself deep asleep, yet awake—a very paradoxical experience, but of great benefit.

Once you have seen your dream disappearing because you have become aware of the dream, your quality of consciousness will have a new flavor to it. The next morning you will wake up with a totally different quality you had never known before. You will wake up for the first time. Now you will know that all those other mornings were false; you were not really awake. The dreams continued—the only difference was that in the night you were dreaming with eyes closed, in the day you were dreaming with eyes open.

But if the dream has disappeared because awareness happened, suddenly you became aware in the dream. . . . And remember, awareness and dreaming cannot exist together. Here, awareness arises, and there, the dream disappears. When you become awake in your sleep, the next morning is going to be something so important that it is incomparable. Nothing like it has ever happened. Your eyes will be so clear, so transparent, and everything will look so psychedelic, so colorful, so alive. Even rocks will be felt to be breathing, pulsating; even rocks will have a heartbeat. When you are awake, the whole existence changes its quality.

We are living in a dream. We are asleep, even when we think we are awake.

7 of Water: Projections

You never look at things as they are; you mix them with your illusions.

And you are so afraid to look straight because you know, unconsciously, deep down somewhere, you know that things are not as you see them.

You think if you look at the reality of things it will be too much, too heavy—you may not be able to stand it. You mix it with dreams just to make it a little sweeter. You think it is bitter so you coat it with sugar. You coat a person in dreams and you feel the person has become sweet? No, you are simply deceiving yourself, nobody else. Hence so much misery. It is out of your dreams that the misery has happened, and one has to be aware of this phenomenon. Don't throw responsibility on the other, otherwise you will create other dreams. See that it is you who are projecting—but it is difficult to look.

In a theater, in a cinema hall, you look at the screen, you never look at the back of the theater—the projector is at the back. The film is not there really on the screen; on the screen it is just a projection of shadow and light. The film exists just at the back, but you never look at that. The projector is there.

Your mind is at the back of so many things, and the mind is the projector. But you always look at the other because the other is the screen. When you are in love the person seems beautiful, no comparison. When you hate, the same person seems to be the ugliest, and you never become aware of how the same person can be the ugliest and was the most beautiful.

When you are in love, the person is a flower, a rose, a rose garden with no thorns. When you dislike, when you hate, the flowers disappear. There are only thorns, no more garden—the ugliest, the dirtiest, you would not like even to look. And you never become aware of what you are doing. How can roses disappear so soon, in a single minute? Not even a gap of a single minute is needed! This moment you are in love and the next moment you are in hate; the same person, the same screen, and the whole story changes.

Just watch and you will be able to see that this person is not the point, you are projecting something. When you project love the person looks lovely, when you project hate the person looks ugly. The person doesn't exist; you have not seen the real person at all.

You cannot see the reality through the eyes of the mind. If you really want to know what the truth is, scriptures won't help. Neither will going to the Himalayas be of any help. Only one thing can help and that is to start looking at things without the mind. Look at the flower and don't allow the mind to say anything. Just look at it. It is difficult because of an old habit of interpreting.

Mulla Nasruddin asked the court for a divorce. He said to the judge, "Now it is impossible. Every day I come back home and I find my wife is hiding some man or other in the closet."

Even the judge was shocked and he said, "Every day?"

Nasruddin said, "Every day! And not the same person either—every day a new person."

Just to console Nasruddin the judge said, "Then you must be very hurt. You come home tired and you think the wife must be waiting for you, to receive and welcome you and be loving. And you come home and you find a new man is hiding in the closet every day!"

Nasruddin said, "Yes, I feel very hurt—because I never have any space to hang my clothes."

It depends on the mind how you interpret things.

So the only way to reach to truth is to learn to be immediate in your vision, to drop the help of the mind. . . . This agency of the mind is the problem, because mind can create only dreams. So what to do?

Try in small things not to bring the mind in. You look at a flower—

you simply look. You don't say, "Beautiful! Ugly!" You don't say anything. Don't bring words in; don't verbalize, simply look. The mind will feel uncomfortable, uneasy. The mind would like to say something. You simply say to the mind, "Be silent! Let me see. I will just look."

In the beginning it will be difficult, but start with things in which you are not too much involved. It will be difficult to look at your wife without bringing words in. You are too much involved, too much emotionally attached. Angry or in love, but too much involved.

Look at things that are neutral—a rock, a flower, a tree, the sun rising, a bird in flight, a cloud moving in the sky. Just look at things with which you are not much involved, from which you can remain detached, to which you can remain indifferent. Start from neutral things and only then move towards emotionally loaded situations.

By and by one becomes efficient. It is just like swimming: in the beginning you feel afraid and in the beginning you cannot believe that you will survive. And you have been working with the mind so long you cannot think that without the mind you can exist for a single moment. But try!

And the more you put the mind aside, the more light will happen to you, because when there are no dreams, doors are open, windows are open, and the sky reaches to you, and the sun rises and it comes to the very heart, the light reaches you. You become more and more filled with truth as you are less and less filled with dreaming.

8 of Water: Letting Go

When the ocean has called you, trust it—take a jump and disappear into it.

The essence of faith or trust is letting go. The fearful person can never let go. He is always on the defense, he is always protecting himself. He is always fighting, he is always antagonistic. Even his prayer, his meditation is nothing but a strategy to protect himself.

The man of faith knows how to let go, the man of faith knows how to surrender. The man of faith knows how to flow with the river and not to push it. He goes with the stream wherever it takes him. He has that courage and confidence that he can go with the stream.

A fearful person is incapable of surrender, although he thinks it is because he is so strong that he cannot surrender. Nobody likes to feel that he is weak; particularly the weaklings never like it. They don't want to come to the realization that they are weak, that they are cowardly. They think they are very strong—they can't surrender.

My own observation is the stronger the person, the easier is the surrender. Only the strong man can surrender, because he trusts himself, he is confident of himself, he knows that he can let go. He is unafraid. He is ready to explore the unknown, he is ready to go into the uncharted; he is thrilled by the journey of the unknown. He wants to taste it, whatsoever the cost and whatsoever the risk. He wants to live in danger.

A man of faith always lives in danger. Danger is his shelter, insecurity is his security, and a tremendous, inquiring quest is his only love. He wants to explore, he wants to go to the very end of existence, or to the very depth of existence, or to the very height of existence. He wants to know what it is—"What is it that surrounds me? What is it that I go on calling 'I'? Who am I?"

A strong person is ready to surrender. He knows that there is no need to fear. "I belong to existence, I am not a stranger here. Existence has mothered me, existence can't be inimical to me. Existence has brought me here, I am a product of existence. Existence has some destiny to fulfill through me."

The strong person always feels that destiny is there: "I am here to do something that is needed by the existence and nobody else can do it except me, otherwise why should I be created?" So he is always ready to go into the dark, to search, to seek.

There are things that can be achieved through effort, but there are also things that can never be achieved through effort. The things that can be achieved through effort are always mundane—money, power, prestige; and the things that cannot be achieved through effort are always sublime—love, prayer, meditation, godliness, truth.

All that is really significant always comes as grace. You have only to become capable of receiving it. You cannot achieve it, you can only receive it. You cannot make any positive effort toward it. Our hands are very small, our reach is not great, but we can wait—and we can wait with great expectancy, although without expectations. We can wait throbbing tremendously, pulsating. In that waiting the beyond penetrates, eternity penetrates into time; the sky comes to the earth.

One has to learn how to wait. One has to learn how to be effortless, one has to learn how to be in a state of surrender. One has to learn how to be in a let-go. The greatest secret in life is the secret of let-go, of surrender, of trusting existence.

All that is great always comes as a gift. Don't strive for it, otherwise you will miss.

One should be overflowing with energy. One should be at ease, but not lazy. One should be relaxed, but not lazy.

Mind tends to be lazy—all laziness is in the mind. Mind wants to avoid any effort. That's why mind does not want to move in new dimensions. It remains clinging to the old, to the familiar, because it knows it is very efficient there. It has a certain proficiency and skill. Now, once you have settled, you don't want to change it.

Many people go on living with a woman or with a man not because they love the man or the woman, but just because it is familiar. Now it will again be a trouble to move with another woman and start from ABC. They are simply lazy.

People go on living the way they are living—even if it is miserable, even if nothing comes out of it except anguish, but they continue because at least it is familiar, known; they have become skillful in it. And they can go on sleeping.

Mind is lazy. This laziness is one of the barriers.

Laziness is a negative state. One should be overflowing with energy. One should be at ease, but not lazy. One should be relaxed, but not lazy.

Laziness and easiness look so alike that it is very easy to misunderstand which is which. But laziness always feels a certain guilt, a certain feeling that "I am doing something that I should not be doing," that "I am not participating in existence." Laziness means you have dropped out of the creativity of the universe—you are standing aside while the universe goes on creating, day in, day out.

Take everything with absolute relaxation, with ease. Whether you are doing something or not, that is not the point. You must be overflowing with energy even when you are not doing anything. These trees are not doing anything, but they are overflowing with energy. You can see that in their flowers, in their colors, in their greenery, in their freshness, in their absolute naked beauty in the sunlight, in the dark night under the stars.

Life is not a tension anywhere except in the minds of humanity. To take life with ease, without any tension, without any hurry—that is not laziness, that is easiness.

1o of Water: Harmony

You are just in the middle between death and life—you are neither. So don't cling to life and don't be afraid of death.

Heraclitus says, "The hidden harmony is better than the obvious."

Have you watched a river? Sometimes it is going left, sometimes it is going right, sometimes to the south, sometimes to the north, and you will see that this river is very inconsistent—but there is a hidden harmony; it reaches the ocean. Wherever it is going, the ocean is the goal. Sometimes it has to move toward the south because the slope is towards the south; sometimes it has to move just the opposite way, towards the north, because the slope is toward the north—but in every direction it is finding the same goal. It is moving towards the ocean, and you will see that it has reached.

Think of a river that is consistent, that says, "I will always move to the south because how can I move to the north? People will say I am inconsistent." This river will never reach the ocean. The rivers of Aristotle never reach the ocean; they are too consistent, too much on the surface. And they don't know the hidden harmony—that through opposites you can seek the same goal. The same goal can be sought through the opposites. That possibility is completely unknown to them.

That possibility is there. Heraclitus says, "The hidden harmony is better than the obvious"—but it is difficult, you will be in constant difficulty. People expect consistency, and the hidden harmony is not a part of the society. It is part of the cosmos but not of the society. Society is a man-made affair, and society has worked out the whole plan as if everything is static. Society has created moralities, codes, as if everything is unmoving. That's why moralities continue for centuries together. Everything changes and the dead rules continue. Everything goes on changing and the so-called moralists always go on preaching the same things that are absolutely irrelevant—but they are consistent with the past. Absolutely irrelevant things go on. . . .

A moralist is a person who lives on the surface. He lives for the rules, the rules are not made for him. He is for the scriptures, the scriptures are not for him. He follows the rules but he doesn't follow awareness. If you follow awareness, witnessing, you will attain to a hidden harmony. Then you are not bothered by the opposite, you can use it. And once you can use the opposite, you have a secret key.

You can make your love more beautiful through hate. Hate is not the enemy of love, it is the very salt that makes love beautiful—it is the background. Then you can make your compassion intense through anger; then it is not the opposite. And this is the meaning of Jesus when he says, "Love your enemies." This is the meaning: Love your enemies because enemies are not enemies—they are friends, you can use them. In a hidden harmony they fall together and become one.

Anger is the enemy—use it, make it a friend! Hate is the enemy—use it, make it a friend! Allow your love to grow deeper through it, make it a soil—it becomes a soil.

This is the hidden harmony: Love the enemy, use the opposite. The opposite is not the opposite, it is just the background.

Death and life are not two, either. Death cannot be really the opposite. If the name of the bow is life, then the name of the lyre must be death. And between these two the fairest harmony of life comes up.

You are just in the middle between death and life—you are neither. So don't cling to life and don't be afraid of death. Heraclitus says, "You are the music between the lyre and the bow. You are the clash and the meeting and the merging, and the harmony, and the fairest that is born out of it."

Don't choose! If you choose, you will be wrong. If you choose, you will become attached to one, identified with one. Don't choose! Let life be the bow, let death be the lyre—and you be the harmony, the hidden harmony.

THE SUIT OF CLOUDS
(SWORDS)

Knowledge—Thoughts—Mind

All your thoughts are given by others to you. Watch—can you find a single thought that is yours, authentically yours, that you have given birth to? They are all borrowed. The sources may be known or unknown, but they are all borrowed. The mind functions like a computer, but before the computer can give you any answer you have to feed it. Mind is a biocomputer.

Knowledge

Life is such a mystery, no one can understand it, and one who claims that he understands it is simply ignorant. He is not aware of what he is saying, what nonsense he is talking. If you are wise, this will be the first realization: life cannot be understood. Understanding is impossible. Only this much can be understood—that understanding is impossible.

Life is not a riddle. A riddle can be solved. A mystery is unsolvable by its very nature—there is no way to solve it. Socrates said, "When I was young, I thought I knew much. When I became old, ripe in wisdom, I came to understand that I knew nothing."

It is reported of one of the Sufi masters, Junnaid, that he was working with a new young man. The young man was not aware of Junnaid's inner wisdom, and Junnaid lived such an ordinary life that it needed very penetrating eyes to realize that you were near a buddha. He worked like an ordinary laborer, and only those who had eyes would recognize him. To recognize Buddha was very easy—he was sitting under a bodhi tree. To recognize Junnaid was very difficult—he was working like a laborer, not sitting under a bodhi tree. He was in every way absolutely ordinary.

One young man was working with him, and that young man was continually showing off his knowledge. So whatsoever Junnaid would do, he would say, "This is wrong. This can be done in this way, it will be better"—he knew about everything. Finally Junnaid laughed and said, "Young man, I am not young enough to know so much."

This is really something. He said, "I am not young enough to know so much." Only a young man can be so foolish, so inexperienced. Socrates was right when he said, "When I was young, I knew too much. When I became ripened, experienced, I came to realize only one thing—that I was absolutely ignorant."

Life is a mystery. That means it cannot be solved. And when all efforts to solve it prove futile, the mystery dawns upon you. Then the doors are open; then you are invited. As a knower, nobody enters the divine. As a child, ignorant, not knowing at all, the mystery embraces you. With a knowing mind you are clever, not innocent. Innocence is the door.

A disciple went to a Zen master and said, "In what state of mind should I seek the truth?" The master said, "There is no mind so there cannot be any state of mind."

Mind is the illusion that is not, but appears to be, and appears to be so much that you think that you *are* the mind. Mind is *maya*, mind is just a dream. Mind is just a projection, a soap bubble floating on a river. The sun is just rising, the rays penetrate the bubble; a rainbow is created and nothing is there in it. When you touch the bubble it is broken and everything disappears—the rainbow, the beauty . . . nothing is left.

Only emptiness becomes one with the infinite emptiness. Just a wall was there, a bubble wall. Your mind is just a bubble wall—prick it, and the mind disappears.

Mind

The master said, "There is no mind, so what type of state are you asking about?" It is difficult to understand. People say, "We would like to attain a silent state of mind." They think that the mind can be silent. Mind can never be silent. Mind means the turmoil, the illness, the disease. Mind means the tense, the anguished state. The mind cannot be silent. When there is silence there is no mind. When silence comes, mind disappears; when mind is there, silence is no more. So there cannot be any "silent mind," just as there cannot be any "healthy disease." Is it possible to have a healthy disease? When health is there, disease disappears.

Silence is the inner health; mind is the inner disease, the inner disturbance.

So there cannot be any silent mind, and this disciple is asking, "What type, what sort, what state of mind should I achieve?" Point blank, the master said, "There is no mind, so you cannot achieve any state." So please drop this illusion; don't try to achieve any state in the illusion. It's as if you are thinking to travel on the rainbow and you ask, "What steps should we take to travel on the rainbow?" I say, "There is no rainbow. The rainbow is just an appearance, so no steps can be taken on it." A rainbow simply appears to exist; it is not really there. It is not a reality, it is a false interpretation of the reality.

The mind is not your reality; it is a false interpretation. You are not the mind, you have never been a mind, you can never be the mind. That is the problem—you have become identified with something that is not. You are like a beggar who believes that he has a kingdom. He is so worried about the kingdom—how to manage it, how to govern it, how to prevent anarchy. There is no kingdom, but he is worried.

Chuang Tzu once dreamt that he had become a butterfly. In the morning he was very depressed. His friends asked, "What has happened? We have never seen you so depressed."

Chuang Tzu said, "I am in a puzzle, I am at a loss, I cannot understand. In the night, while asleep, I dreamt that I had become a butterfly."

So the friends laughed: "Nobody is ever disturbed by dreams. When you awake, the dream has disappeared, so why are you disturbed?"

Chuang Tzu said, "That is not the point. Now I am puzzled: if Chuang Tzu can become a butterfly in the dream, it is possible that now the butterfly has gone to sleep and is dreaming that she is Chuang Tzu."

If Chuang Tzu can become a butterfly in the dream, why not the other? The butterfly can dream and become Chuang Tzu. So what is real—Chuang Tzu dreaming that he has become a butterfly or the butterfly dreaming that she has become Chuang Tzu? What is real? Rainbows are there, you can become a butterfly in a dream. And you have become a mind in this bigger dream you call life.

When you awaken you don't achieve an awakened state of mind, you achieve a no-state of mind, you achieve no-mind.

Thoughts

What does no-mind mean? It is difficult to follow but sometimes, unknowingly, you have achieved it. You may not have recognized it. Sometimes, just sitting ordinarily, not doing anything, there is no thought in the mind—because mind is just the process of thinking. It is not a substance, it is just a procession. You could say a crowd has gathered, but is there really something like a crowd? Is a crowd substantial, or are there only individuals? By and by the individuals will go away, then will there be a crowd left behind? When individuals have gone, there is no crowd.

The mind is just like a crowd; thoughts are the individuals. And because thoughts are there continuously, you think the process is substantial. Drop each individual thought and finally nothing is left. There is no mind as such, only thinking.

Thoughts are moving so fast that you cannot see the interval between two thoughts. But the interval is always there. *That interval is you.* In that interval there is neither Chuang Tzu nor the butterfly—because the butterfly is a sort of mind and Chuang Tzu is also a sort of mind. A butterfly is one combination of thoughts, Chuang Tzu a different combination, but both are minds. When the mind is not there, who are you—Chuang Tzu or a butterfly? Neither. And what is the state? Are you in an enlightened state of mind? If you think you are in an enlightened state of mind this is, again, a thought, and when *thought* is there *you* are not. If you feel that you are a buddha, this is a thought. The mind has entered; now the process is there, again the sky is clouded, the blueness lost. The infinite blueness you can see no more.

Between two thoughts, try to be alert. Look into the interval, the space in between. You will see no-mind; that is your nature. Thoughts come and go—they are accidental—but that inner space always remains. Clouds gather and go, disappear—they are accidental—but the sky remains.

You are the sky.

King of Clouds: Control

In controlling yourself you miss the whole point of being alive, because you miss celebration. How can you celebrate if you are too controlled?

Don't try to become anything—patient, loving, non-violent, peaceful. Don't try. If you try, you will force yourself and you will become a hypocrite. That's how the whole of religion has turned into hypocrisy. Inside you are different; on the outside painted. You smile, and inside you would have liked to kill. Inside you carry all the rubbish and on the outside you go on sprinkling perfume. Inside you stink; on the outside you create an illusion as if you are a rose flower.

Never repress. Repression is the greatest calamity that has happened to man. And it has happened for very beautiful reasons. You look at a buddha—so silent, undisturbed. A greed arises: you would also like to be like him. What to do? You start trying to be a stone statue. Whenever there is a situation and you can be disturbed, you hold yourself back. You control yourself.

Control is a dirty word. It has not four letters in it, but it is a four-letter word.

And when I talk about freedom I don't mean license. When I say freedom you may understand license, because that's how things go. A controlled mind, whenever it hears about freedom, immediately understands it as license. License is the opposite pole of control. Freedom is just in between, just exactly in the middle, where there is no control and no license.

Freedom has its own discipline, but it is not enforced by any authority. It comes out of your awareness, out of authenticity. Freedom should never be misunderstood as license, otherwise you will again miss.

Awareness brings freedom. In freedom there is no need for control, because there is no possibility for license. It is because of license that you have been forced to control, and if you remain licentious the society will go on controlling you.

It is because of your licentiousness that the policeman exists and the judge and the politician and the courts, and they go on forcing you to control yourself. And in controlling yourself you miss the whole point of being alive, because you miss celebration. How can you celebrate if you are too controlled?

You can choose either control or license. You can say, "If I drop control, I will become licentious. If I drop license then I have to become controlled." But I tell you, if you become aware, control and license both go down the same drain. They are two aspects of the same coin, and in awareness they are not needed.

Queen of Clouds: Morality

There is no higher law than love, so love is the true foundation of morality—not codes, not commandments.

The righteous, the moralistic, the puritanical are always ready to condemn, to send more and more people to hell, to crucify people, to kill and destroy.

The moralist is ready to suffer, he is ready to be a masochist, he is ready to go through all kinds of foolish austerities just to enjoy the feeling of superiority, the feeling of holier-than-thou, the feeling that "You are all sinners and I am a saint."

The real saint has a totally different quality. He is not moralistic; he knows how to forgive, because he knows he has been forgiven so much. He knows human limitations, because he himself has suffered through those human limitations. He can forgive, he is understanding.

The moralist is never understanding, he is never forgiving; he cannot forgive because he has been so hard with himself. He has attained to his so-called character with such difficulty that the only joy, the only pleasure that he can get is that of holier-than-thou. How can he forgive? If he forgives then he cannot enjoy the egoistic trip that he has been on.

Morality is a social phenomenon; society needs it because society consists of millions of people. It has to keep a certain order, a certain discipline; otherwise there will be chaos. Morality keeps that order. Morality creates a conscience in you. Conscience functions as an inner policeman who does not allow you to do anything that is against the law or against the code or against the tradition. Society has imprinted in your heart certain ideas and now you are dominated by those ideas. Even if you go against those ideas they will torture you, they will become a nightmare to you. If you follow them you will feel you are not tortured so much.

So the immoral person finds himself in two difficulties. One comes from the outside because he starts losing people's respect; and in this world respect is the most valuable thing in people's eyes because it is a nourishment for the ego. The moment you lose respect your ego starts dying, your ego is hurt, your ego is wounded. Secondly, something inside you starts creating an inner torture for you—your conscience. That conscience is also created by the same society.

Hence, society pressures you from both sides, outer and inner. You are just crushed between these two rocks. So cowards cannot be immoral people; cowards are always moral people. In fact they are not moral but only cowards! Because they are cowards they cannot be immoral—that is too dangerous, too risky.

And the moral people, the so-called moral people, live a superficial life. They are bound to live a superficial life because their conscience is not their own—what else can be their own? They don't possess even their own conscience, what else can they possess? They are the poorest people in the world.

And they are not moral because they understand the beauty of being moral; they are moral simply because they don't have guts enough to be immoral. They follow the dictates of society and conscience just out of fear. There is fear of the law and there is fear of hell; there is fear of the policeman and there is fear of God. They are constantly trembling, their life is nothing but a constant trembling. Their prayers arise out of that trembling—naturally those prayers are false; they are fear-oriented. Even their conception of God is nothing but a projection of their fear.

That's why these people are rightly called "God-fearing" people. They are not God-loving people. And remember, one who fears God can never love God. And one who loves God need never fear God. Fear and love can't exist together; it is impossible. Their coexistence is not possible in the nature of things.

But society pays you enough to be moral, gives you as much ego as it is possible to give—not only here but in the afterworld too. There are also places, special places reserved for you in heaven. The sinner is suffering here and the sinner will suffer in hell too, and the so-called saint is respected here and he is going to be respected in the other world too.

This is a strategy, a very subtle psychological strategy of society to exploit you. But because of this strategy you have completely lost track of real morality—a morality that is not dictated by fear, a morality that does not arise out of cowardice, a morality that is not fear-oriented.

A totally different vision of morality has been given by the buddhas, by the awakened ones of all the ages. Their vision is that real morality comes not out of conscience but out of consciousness. Become more conscious, release more conscious energy in your being, explode into consciousness—and then you will see you are living a life in absolute attunement with existence. Sometimes it may be in tune with society and sometimes it may not be in tune with society, because society itself is not always in tune with existence.

Whenever society is in tune with existence you will be in tune with society; whenever society is not in tune with existence you will not be in tune with society. But the real moral person never cares, he is even ready to risk his life. Socrates did that, Jesus did that. Buddha was constantly living in danger. This has always been the case, for the simple reason that they were living according to their own light.

If it fits with society, good; if it does not fit with society it is bad for society but it has nothing to do with you. Society has to change itself. Socrates is not going to change himself, Jesus is not going to change himself according to society, Buddha is not going to live according to the crowd. The crowd consists of blind people, of utterly unconscious people who are fast asleep, who know nothing of themselves. To follow them is the most stupid thing in the world that a man can do. One should be intelligent enough to wake up one's own consciousness.

Real religion consists not of conscience but of consciousness. Religion really consists in creating a different kind of morality—not the so-called ordinary morality, but a morality that is spontaneous, a morality that arises by itself and is not imposed, a morality that is a consequence of your own intelligence.

Knight of Clouds: Fighting

In the fight you can create the notion of the ego; in the challenge, in resistance, you can create the notion of the ego. If you drop fighting and you float with the stream, by and by you will come to know that you do not exist separate from the whole.

Everybody is going upstream, trying to fight with the river—why? Because in the fight you can create the notion of the ego; in the challenge, in resistance, you can create the notion of the ego. If you drop fighting and you float with the stream, by and by you will come to know that you do not exist separate from the whole. That's why people love challenge, people love danger, people want to fight. If there is nobody to fight they will create something or other to fight, because only in fighting can their ego be maintained. And it has to be maintained continuously; it is just like a bicycle—you pedal it, and you have to go on pedaling otherwise it will fall. You have to continuously pedal it.

The ego needs continuous pedaling. Every moment you have to go on fighting with something or other. Once you stop fighting, suddenly you find the cycle has fallen. The ego cannot exist without the fight.

Never compel anybody to do something and never compel yourself to do something; let things happen, then existence will be doing them through you. There are two ways of doing things: one, you do; another, existence does them through you. If you do them, you create anxiety for yourself, anguish, misery, because then you become result oriented; you think, "Am I going to succeed or not?" You become more concerned with the end result than with the process. And then you are constantly worried; and whatever happens you will be frustrated.

If you succeed you will be frustrated because the success will not deliver the goods that you were thinking were going to be delivered by it. If you fail, of course you will be in misery.

People who fail are in misery and people who have succeeded are in misery. In fact those who have succeeded are more in misery than those who have failed because a failure can still hope. A man who has really succeeded cannot hope. He becomes absolutely hopeless. Now he has nowhere to go, he has succeeded—ask the very rich people why they are in such misery. A poor man we can understand, but why are rich people in so much misery? They have succeeded and now, being successful, they have come to realize that it has been useless, that success has not given them anything. It has simply wasted their whole life.

Failure fails, success fails. There is only one possibility: that you know your being. Only that can satisfy, only that never fails. But that is not part of "becoming." That has nothing to do with time. Right now, this very moment, it is available. It is already there in its total glory. The king is on the throne within you but you never look there. You are in search of money, knowledge, prestige, power, and you go out. And, to all those who go out I say—come in!

Drop learning, learn unlearning. Come in! Drop the doer; learn how to do things without doing them. This is the greatest secret of all, the greatest miracle that can happen to anybody—you simply become a passage, a vehicle, a hollow flute, and songs start flowing through you.

Just don't come between you and yourself. Please, put yourself aside, don't get in the way. If you can learn only one thing, how to stand aside, you have learned all. And then you become aware that everything is going on by itself. The whole is working. The part is not needed to work, it only needs to participate. It only needs not to create trouble and conflict. It only needs to be with the whole.

Page of Clouds: Mind

Don't be cunning and calculating. Don't try to be clever; the more clever you are, the more miserable you will be. This existence can be contacted only in innocence, childlike innocence.

All your cleverness will lead you into falsities, new falsities, again and again. One has to drop being clever. See the point, that's what Jesus means when he says, "Unless you are like small children, you will not enter into the kingdom." He is saying, drop your cleverness. Don't be cunning and calculating. Don't try to be clever; the more clever you are, the more miserable you will be. This existence can be contacted only in innocence, childlike innocence. Your knowledge is not going to help, only your innocence.

Function from the state of not knowing, never function from the state of knowing.

The knowledgeable person is the closed person—and you have all become knowledgeable. You have read books, scriptures, you have been taught in the church, in the college, school, university; you have accumulated much knowledge. Now you go functioning from this knowledge that you have accumulated, and it is all borrowed—it has no roots in you. It is all rubbish, but you go on sitting on top of it. It gives you ego, certainly. The bigger heap you have of knowledge, the higher the peak of it you sit on. You go on exhibiting your degrees, you go on throwing your knowledge all around, you are continuously making others feel that they don't know as much as you know.

The less people know, the more stubbornly they know it. The stupid person is one who has become very stubborn about borrowed things—very stubborn about his Christianity, about his Hinduism, about this and that—very stubborn. The less people know, the more stubbornly they know it. Stubbornness is the indication of a stupid man. He is closed. He may be a great pundit, a great scholar, but that doesn't make any difference; he is closed. He is surrounded by his knowledge—not even a small aperture is left for existence to enter him. His heart becomes unavailable. He lives surrounded by a wall; he walls people out. And the wall is made of knowledge—very subtle, the bricks almost invisible.

The more you understand, the less you realize that you know. When understanding grows, knowledge starts disappearing—in the same proportion. The more understanding you become, the less knowledgeable you are. And the ultimate in knowing is absolute ignorance, innocence, childlike purity.

Yes, Socrates is right when he says, "I know only one thing: that I don't know anything at all." Remember it: spiritual perception opens up only when you have dropped all principles. This is the essential message of Zen. Get rid of principles. Don't be confined by any philosophy, by any guesswork, however clever it is. Remember only one thing, that unless something is your experience it is not worth keeping. Drop it.

Don't gather rubbish, don't gather unnecessary luggage. This is my observation of thousands of people: I see them carrying such great psychological luggage, and for no reason at all. They go on gathering anything they come across. They read the newspaper and they will gather some crap from it. They will talk to people and they will gather some crap. They go on gathering . . . and if they start stinking . . . no wonder!

Just observe what kind of thoughts go on inside your mind. Just one day sit, close your doors, and write down for half an hour whatever is passing in your mind, and you will understand what I mean. . . . Just write for half an hour, and you will be surprised what goes on inside your mind. It remains in the background, it is constantly there; it surrounds you like a cloud. With this cloud you cannot know reality; you cannot attain to spiritual perception.

This cloud has to be dropped. And it is just with your decision to drop it that it will disappear. You are clinging to it—the cloud is not interested in you, remember.

Ace of Clouds: Consciousness

If you understand it, the world is a great device to make you more conscious.

Your enemy is your friend, and the curses are blessings, and the misfortunes can be turned into fortunes. It depends only on one thing: if you know the key of awareness.

When somebody insults you, that is the moment to keep alert. When your wife looks at somebody else and you feel hurt, that is the moment to keep alert. When you are feeling sad, gloomy, depressed, when you feel the whole world is against you, that is the moment to be alert. When you are surrounded by a dark night, that is the moment to keep your light burning. And all these situations will prove helpful—they are meant for it.

I don't believe what others call meditation, that ten minutes or twenty minutes you do it and then just be your ordinary self for twenty-four hours, and then again for twenty minutes meditate. This is stupid. It is like saying to a person, "Every day in the morning for twenty minutes, breathe. And then forget all about it, because you have to do many other things. The next morning you can breathe again."

To me, meditation is exactly like breathing. So whatever you are doing and wherever you are, do things more consciously. For example, you can raise your hand without any consciousness, just unconsciously, out of habit. But you can raise your hand with full awareness. And you can see the difference between the two. The act is the same: one is mechanical, another is full of consciousness and the quality is tremendously different.

Try it, because it is a question of taste and experience. Walking, just try for a few minutes to walk consciously; be alert each step and you will be surprised that the quality of your walk is totally different, it is relaxed. There is no tension and there is a subtle joy that is arising out of your relaxed walking. And the more you become aware of this joy, the more you would like to be awake.

Eating, eat with awareness. People are simply throwing food into their mouths, not even chewing it, just swallowing it. Millions of people in America are suffering from overeating. Strange world we are living in: one thousand people are dying every day in Ethiopia because they don't have food, and millions of people are dying in America because they have too much food. These people who are suffering from obesity, fatness, cannot resist eating more and more. No doctor can help them unless they become aware while they are eating.

If they become aware, a few things happen as a by-product. Their eating will be slowed down. They will start chewing, because unless you chew your food you are putting an unnecessary burden on your whole system. Your stomach has no teeth. One has to chew forty-two times each bite, then anything that you are eating becomes liquid. A man of awareness only drinks, because before he swallows he has changed that solid food into liquid. And when you are chewing forty-two times, you are enjoying the taste so much. One bite taken by an unconscious man gives forty-two times more taste to the conscious man. It is simple arithmetic: the unconscious man will have to eat forty-two bites just to have the same taste—and then he becomes fat, and still unsatisfied. Still he feels the need to eat more. The man of awareness eats only as much as his body needs. He immediately feels that now there is no need, the hunger is gone, he is content.

Meditation has to be spread all over your twenty-four hours. Even falling asleep, remain alert to how sleep is descending on you, so slowly, so silently, but you can hear its steps. The darkness is growing, you are relaxing—you can feel the muscles, the body, the tensions that are preventing the sleep—and soon you will see the whole body has relaxed and the sleep has come. Slowly, slowly, a great revolution happens. Sleep comes to you, but something deep inside you goes on remaining awake, even in sleep.

2 of Clouds: Schizophrenia

Schizophrenia is not a disease that happens to a few people—it is the normal state of humanity. Everybody is divided, split.

One scientist, B. F. Skinner, did an experiment worth remembering. A white mouse was starved for two or three days so it was very hungry; really, the mouse was just hunger, ready to jump and eat anything available. Then it was put on a platform. Just below the platform there were two similar boxes, the same color, same size, and both boxes contained food. The white mouse could jump in either the right box or the left.

The mouse immediately jumped, not even a single moment of thought. But whenever he jumped into the right box, he would get an electric shock. And there was a trapdoor, so he would fall inside another box through the trapdoor and would not be able to reach the food. Whenever he jumped into the left box, there was no shock and there was no trapdoor, so he would reach the food. Within two or three days he learned the trick: he would jump in the left box and avoid the right.

Then Skinner made a change, he changed the places of the boxes. The mouse jumped into the left box and found that there was an electric shock. Now it was disturbed, confused as to what to do and what not to do. So before jumping it would tremble and waver, doubtful.

This is how a philosopher is—a white mouse, trembling, doubtful what to do: left or right, and how to choose? And who knows. . . ? But then it got accustomed again.

Then Skinner again made a change. The mouse became so confused that although it was hungry it would wait, trembling, looking at this box and that—and how to decide? Then he decided the thing you have decided: he jumped between the two boxes—but there was no food, this was not going to help. And after a few weeks of experiment, the white mouse went mad, neurotic.

This is what is happening to you: you have become confused— what to do, what not to do? And the only thing that comes to the mind is that if it is difficult to choose this, difficult to choose that, then it is better to make a compromise, just jump in the middle.

But there is no food. Of course, there is no electric shock, but there is no food either.

You miss life if you jump in the middle. If it were possible for the white mouse to mount both boxes, he would have done that. These are the two possibilities that open for reasoning: mount both horses or just jump in the middle.

Intelligence, a very penetrating and keen intelligence is needed to understand the problem—there is no other solution. I am not going to give you any solution; just the understanding of the problem is the solution. You understand the problem and the problem disappears.

Schizophrenia is not a disease that happens to a few people—it is the normal state of humanity. Everybody is divided, split. You can watch it in your own life. When you are not with a woman, with a man, not in love, you think, you fantasize about love. Love seems to be the goal.

That seems to be the very meaning of life. When you are with a woman or with a man and in love, suddenly you start thinking in terms of spirituality: "This is attachment, this is possessiveness, this is lust." A condemnation arises.

You cannot be alone and you cannot be with somebody. If you are alone you hanker for the crowd, for the other. If you are with somebody you start hankering to be alone. This is something to be understood, because everybody has to face this problem. You are born in a schizophrenic world. You have been given double standards. You have been taught materialism, and you have been taught spirituality, together. The whole society goes on teaching you contradictory things. You are born in a schizophrenic world. Your parents were schizophrenic, your teachers were schizophrenic, your priests, your politicians are schizophrenic. They go on talking about two diametrically opposite goals, and they go on creating the split in you.

3 of Clouds: Ice-olation

You have to dissolve the ego, not to isolate it. . . . If you want to renounce anything, renounce yourself.

These three words have to be remembered: dependence, independence, and interdependence. Dependent you are; independence you seek; interdependence I teach.

Dependent you are, because everywhere you will feel you are dependent, everywhere a limitation comes in. If you love somebody, you become dependent on him or on her. Everywhere life brings dependence. Then the idea arises that in the world you can never be independent, so escape from the world. You can escape, but you can never be independent; you can only be deceived. Even in the Himalayas you are not independent. You are still dependent on the sun. If the sun does not rise, you will be dead immediately. You will be dependent on the oxygen and air: if the oxygen disappears, you will be dead. You will be dependent on water; you will be dependent on a thousand and one things.

Dependence has to be understood, not avoided. If you understand dependence, you will understand immediately that hidden behind it is interdependence. Dependence is just a misinterpretation. Those who have understood it know that you are not only dependent on the sun, the sun is also dependent on you. Without you the sun cannot exist, as you cannot exist without the sun. Even a small blade of grass will be missed from existence; the existence will never be complete without it. There will be a gap, something missing.

So don't think that the stars are great and a blade of grass is very small and tiny. In existence, nothing is great and nothing is small, because existence is one.

This is what is meant by ecology: interdependence. And ecology is not only of this earth, it is of the totality. Ecology is a spiritual phenomenon.

Most people interpret interdependence as dependence. That is a wrong notion, and because of that wrong notion, a wrong desire arises: how to be independent. Out of one error another error arises. You cannot be, and if somebody teaches you independence—there are people who teach this—they are teaching sheer stupidity. You are part of, you are one with, the whole. You are a wave in the ocean. The wave cannot be independent. How can you take the wave apart from the ocean? And I tell you, the ocean also cannot be separate from the wave. Without waves the ocean will also disappear. The waves cannot be without the ocean and the ocean cannot be without the waves, because waves are nothing but the ocean waving. Because of language the separation arises. You say the waves and the ocean; in fact, there are not the waves and the ocean, it is all one—the ocean waving. Waves are not things . . . a process, a movement, a breathing of the ocean. You and your breathing are not two things: you are the breathing, the breathing is you. You breathe and the breathing breathes you—they are inseparable.

Life is one. For this oneness, interdependence, god is another name. Love is still another name, and even better than god, because god has been destroyed by the theologians. Love is still pure and virgin.

I don't teach isolation, because I want you to leave the ego, and not the world. The world is not the problem. The world is tremendously beautiful; it is pure joy; nothing is wrong in it. Something is wrong in you, not in the world. Drop the wrongness in you; don't renounce the world.

4 of Clouds: Postponement

Always think of each moment as the last, as if there is going to be no tomorrow at all. Then what will you do?

Start being blissful. Don't postpone it for tomorrow. Don't say, "Tomorrow I will be blissful." That is the sure way to miss it forever. Either now or never. Not even a single moment's postponement is needed. Always think of each moment as the last, as if there is going to be no tomorrow at all. Then what will you do?

Will you remain miserable in this moment if there is going to be no other moment? Will you still persist in being in misery? You will drop the whole thing and you will say, "Let me dance, let me sing, let me be! Enough of all this nonsense, this trivia, this rubbish. . . ." You will forget all the small things that were so important just a moment ago because you were thinking you were going to live forever and ever.

It happened that a great king became very angry with his prime minister—so angry that in a rage he sent the message to him: "This is the last day of your life; tomorrow morning you will be killed." The house of the prime minister was surrounded by the army so he could not escape. But the king was puzzled, because he didn't even try. He was a powerful man, he could have managed some way—but rather than escaping, he invited in all his friends.

When the king heard that they were having a party—dancing and singing and eating and drinking—he himself went to see what was happening. Had the man gone mad? Tomorrow was to be his last day, and the king had never seen the prime minister so happy in his life. He was just vibrating with joy, pulsating, radiating. He was so happy to see the king. He invited the king in and he said, "Come and participate, because this is my last day. I decided: Why waste this day? Why not enjoy it? So I have called all my friends. And you have also come—this is a great blessing. Let us dance and sing, because I will never be again. Tomorrow I disappear . . . let me disappear with dance. We are going to celebrate the whole night!"

The king was so impressed that he hugged the prime minister and forgave him and said, "You have taught me one of the greatest lessons of my life."

This is the way one should live, because each moment is the last, as far as we know, because the next is not certain. So be blissful here and now, be blissful all the way. And once the decision is there, it starts changing your life. Values become different: things that were important up to this moment lose their importance, and things about which you have always thought, "Someday I am going to do them," become important. Anger becomes unimportant; love becomes important. Enmity starts looking meaningless; friendship becomes meaningful.

If one can live in constant remembrance of death, one is bound to become a buddha. Buddha used to send his disciples to the cemetery. The beginners had to go there and to live there for three months so that they could see death continually happening, people being burned. And just the previous day the monk would have seen this man walking so happily on the road, and now he was no more. Day in, day out, people would be brought and would be burned . . . because in India they are burned—and he would see the people disappearing into flames. He had to wait, to sit there for three months watching, watching, seeing how fragile life is, how uncertain the future is, how death is an absolute certainty. And when he would come back after three months he would be a totally different man—his values different, his priorities different.

5 of Clouds: Comparison

When you compare, you miss; then you will always be looking at others.

And no two persons are the same, they cannot be. Every individual is unique and every individual is superior, but this superiority is not comparable.

Once it happened that a disciple came to a Zen master and asked, "Why are a few people so intelligent and a few so stupid? Why are a few people so beautiful and a few so ugly? Why this inconsistency? If God is everywhere, if he is the creator, then why does he create one ugly and another beautiful? And don't talk to me about *karmas*. I have heard all those nonsensical answers—that because of *karmas*, past lives, one is beautiful and another is ugly. I am not concerned with past lives. In the beginning, when there was no yesterday, how did the difference come? Why was one created beautiful and another ugly? And if everyone was created equal, equally beautiful and intelligent, how can they act differently, how can they have different *karmas*?"

The master said, "Wait! This is such a secret thing that I will tell you when everybody has left." So the man sat, eager, but people kept coming and going and there was no chance. By the evening everybody had left, so the man said, "Now?"

And the master said, "Come out with me." The moon was coming up and the master took him in the garden and said, "Look, that tree there is small, this tree here is so tall. I have been living with these trees for many years and they have never raised the question of why that tree is small and this tree is big. I used to ask the same question sitting under these trees. Then my mind dropped, and the question dropped. Now I know. This tree is small and that tree is big; there is no problem. So look! There is no problem."

The mind compares. How can you compare when the mind is not? How can you say this tree is small and that tree big? When the mind drops, comparison drops, and when there is no comparison, the beauty of existence erupts. It becomes a volcanic eruption, it explodes. Then you see the small is big and the big is small; then all contradictions are lost and the inner consistency is seen.

When you feel that you are inferior, when you compare yourself with others and see that they are superior to you, what will you do? The ego feels hurt—you are inferior. You just cannot accept it, so you have to deceive yourself and others.

There is another type of superiority, and that superiority is the absence of inferiority, not the opposite to it. You simply don't compare. When you don't compare, how can you be inferior?

Look: if you are the only person on earth and there is nobody else, will you be inferior? With whom will you compare yourself? Relative to what? If you are alone, what will you be, inferior or superior? You will be neither. You cannot be inferior because no one is above you; you cannot declare yourself superior because there is no one beneath you. You will be neither superior nor inferior.

And I say to you that this is the superiority of the soul. It never compares. Compare, and the inferiority arises. Don't compare, and you simply are—unique.

Be non-ambitious and attain to your intrinsic superiority. It is intrinsic. It doesn't have to be proved or achieved. You already have it, it is already there—it has always been with you and it will always remain with you. Your very being is superior but you don't know what being is there. You don't know who you are. Hence so much effort in seeking your identity, in searching, in proving that you are superior to others. You don't know who you are.

Once you know, then there is no problem. You are already superior. And it is not only you that is superior—everything is superior. The whole of existence is superior without anything being inferior, because existence is one. Neither the inferior nor the superior can exist. The non-ambitious mind comes to realize this.

In fact, everybody is so unique that all comparison is wrong, utterly wrong. But you don't know your uniqueness. You have never entered your own being, you have never encountered yourself. You have never looked in that direction at all. You are bound to feel inferior. Even the greatest people of your history, the people you call very great, all feel inferior in some way or other, maybe different ways of feeling inferior, but nobody can really feel superior—he will be missing something. He may not be so beautiful as somebody else, he may not be so healthy as somebody else, he may not be such a great musician as somebody else. He may be a president of a country, but when it comes to singing, a beggar can make him feel inferior. He may be the president of a country, but may not be so rich. There are thousands of other people who are far richer.

Life consists of millions of things and if you are constantly comparing . . . and that's what you have been told to do. You have been brought up in such a way, educated in such a stupid way that you are constantly comparing. Somebody is taller than you, somebody seems more beautiful than you, somebody seems to be more intelligent than you, somebody seems more virtuous, more religious, more meditative. And you are always in a state of inferiority, suffering.

Look within yourself and you will experience great uniqueness. And all inferiority disappears, evaporates; it was created by you and by wrong education, it was created by a subtle strategy—the strategy of comparison. Once you know your uniqueness you are joyous, and then there is no need to follow anybody. Learn from everybody. An intelligent person even learns from idiots, because there are few things you can learn only from idiots because they are experts in idiocy. At least watching them, observing them, you can avoid a few things in your life.

You can learn from everybody, not only from people but also from animals, from trees, from clouds, from rivers. But there is no question of imitating. You can't become a river, but you can learn some quality that is river-likeness: the flow, the let-go. You can learn something from a rose flower. You cannot become a rose flower, you need not, but you can learn something from the rose. You see the rose so delicate yet so strong in the wind, in the rain, in the sun. By the evening it will be gone but has no care about it, is joyous in the moment. You can learn from the rose how to live in the moment. Right now the rose is dancing in the wind, in the rain, unafraid, unconcerned for the future. By the evening the petals will wither away, but who bothers about the evening? This moment is all and this dance is all there is.

Learn something from the rose. Learn something from the bird on the wing—the courage to go into the unbounded. Learn from all sources but don't imitate. But that is possible only if you have found the right space to begin with, and that is acquaintance with yourself.

6 of Clouds: The Burden

Life is a constant resurrection. Every moment it dies, every moment it is born anew. But you go on carrying the old mind; you will never fit anywhere.

Life is a movement, a constant flux. Each moment it is new. But the mind? The mind is never new. It is always lagging behind. The very nature of the mind is such that it cannot be one with life. Life goes on, mind lags behind. There is always an inconsistency between life and mind—it has to be so.

You see a flower: the moment you realize that you have seen it, it is no longer the same—life has moved. You see a river, but you don't see the same river again. You cannot. Says old Heraclitus, "You cannot step in the same river twice." And I say to you that you cannot step in the same river even once—because the river is constantly flowing.

The moment mind recognizes something, it is already no longer the case. Mind goes on accumulating dead footprints. Life once existed there, but it is there no more.

And we are trained as minds; that is the misery. You go on missing life. And you will go on missing it unless you drop the mind, unless you start living out of a state of no-mind. Then you are one with life. Then the inconsistency between you and your mind disappears. Then you no longer live according to some ideas, because ideas are of the mind. You don't live according to any ideology, religion, scripture, tradition—you simply live out of the emptiness of your being.

It is difficult in the beginning even to conceive how one can live out of emptiness. But out of emptiness all the trees are growing, and out of emptiness stars are moving, and out of emptiness the whole existence exists—and there is no trouble. Only man has the absurd idea that without mind it will be difficult to exist. In fact, with the mind it is difficult to exist—because existence and mind are separate, not only separate but two contrary dimensions. If you want to be consistent with the mind, you will be inconsistent with life.

It happened: There was a case against Mulla Nasruddin in the court, and the judge asked him, "How old are you, Nasruddin?"

And he said, "Of course, you know and everybody knows I am forty years old."

The judge was surprised and he said, "But five years ago also you were in the court and I asked you, and then too you said that you were forty years old. How is it possible? After five years, you are still forty years old?"

Nasruddin said, "I am a consistent man, sir. Once I say I am forty, I will remain forty forever—you can rely on me."

If you are consistent with the mind, you will become such a reliable man. You will be consistent—but absolutely inconsistent—because life goes on. It is never static. Not even for a single moment does life stay anywhere. Life doesn't know any rest. Life has no tradition to follow, no ideology to imitate, no pattern fixed by the past. Life is always an opening into the unknown.

Mind is always enclosed within the experience that has happened already, and life is always open for the experience that has never happened before. How can they meet? How is there any possibility of their meeting? Then, by and by, mind becomes completely enclosed in itself. Not only that, the mind even becomes afraid to see what life is.

The fear comes because the mind knows that if you look at the life, you will be proved wrong. So better remain with closed eyes, don't look at life. Interpret life always according to the mind. Don't listen to life! That's how you have become deaf.

Life is a constant resurrection. Every moment it dies, every moment it is born anew. But you go on carrying the old mind; you will never fit anywhere. And you know it! You never fit anywhere; you never fit with anybody. Wherever you are, there is some trouble.

Something is always missing, lacking. Harmony never comes out of your relationships—because the harmony is possible only if you are a fluxlike phenomenon, changing, moving, merging into the new.

If you become a formless river of consciousness, then everything fits. Then you fit with life, and life fits with you—suddenly everything is absolutely okay.

7 of Clouds: Politics

Our culture, our education, our religion—they all teach us to be hypocrites in such subtle ways that unless you go deep in search, you will never find out what you have been doing.

As you grow up, society goes on teaching you to be this way, to behave this way. You start becoming a hypocrite and you become identified with your hypocrisy.

The man who first made up the maxim, "Honesty is the best policy," must have been a very cunning man. Honesty is not policy; and if it is policy, then it is not honesty. Then you are honest because it pays—you will be dishonest if that pays. Honesty is the best policy if it is paying, but if sometimes it is not paying, then dishonesty of course is the best policy. The question is, which one is going to pay?

There are three words deeply related to one another: policy, politeness, and politics. What is politeness? It is a kind of politics. Both words are derived from the same root. All three words—policy, politeness, politics—have the same root, they all mean the same thing. But politeness you think is a nice quality. You would never think of it in terms of politics, but it is politics. To be polite is a defense measure.

In Europe you shake hands. Why do you shake the right hand? Why not the left? It is really part of politics. To shake hands is nothing friendly. It is just a gesture to demonstrate that "My right hand is empty so don't be worried. And let me see that your right hand also is empty, that there is not a knife or something in it." And when you are shaking right hands you cannot pull your sword out because with the left hand . . . unless you happen to be a leftist! It is just a way of giving certainty to the other person that you are not going to harm him, and he is giving certainty to you that he is not going to harm you. Slowly, it became a gesture of greeting.

In India, you greet the other person with both hands, but that too is simply showing that both your hands are empty. It is far better than shaking hands, because who knows about the left hand? Sometimes even the right hand does not know about the left hand, so it is better to show that both hands are empty. That is far better and far more polite also. But you are saying, "I am completely defenseless. You need not be wary about me or worried about me. You can relax." These are symbols that people have learned.

Our culture, our education, our religion—they all teach us to be hypocrites in such subtle ways that unless you go deeply in search, you will never find out what you have been doing.

Why do you smile when you meet a friend? What is the need? If you are not feeling like smiling, why do you smile? You have to do it. This is a policy that is paying, because some day you may need this man's help, and if you have always been smiling at him, he cannot refuse. If you have never smiled at him and never even said "Hi," then you need not bother even to approach him; he will throw you out of his house with a "Go to hell!"

One has to understand all these layers and detach oneself from all of them.

Become a watcher so that you cannot become identified with any dream.

It is difficult not to abuse one's authority. Very difficult—because in the first place people seek authority just to abuse it.

You have heard Lord Acton's famous dictum that power corrupts. It is not true. His observation is right in a way, but not true. Power never corrupts anybody, but still Lord Acton is right—because we always see people being corrupted by power. How can power corrupt people? But in fact, it is corrupted people who seek power. Of course, when they don't have power, they cannot express their corruption. When they have power, then they are free. Then they can move with the power, then they are not worried. Then they come out in their true light, then they show their real face.

Power never corrupts anybody, but corrupted people are attracted to power. And when they have power, then of course they use it for all their desires and passions.

It happens. A person may be very humble. When he is seeking a political post he may be very humble, and you may know him—you may have known that for his whole life he was a simple and humble person, and you vote for him. The moment he is in power, there is a metamorphosis; he is no longer the same person. People are surprised—how does power corrupt?

In fact, that humbleness was false, bogus. He was humble because he was weak. He was humble because he had no power. He was afraid the powerful people would crush him. His humbleness was his politics, his policy. Now he need not be afraid, now nobody can crush him. Now he can express his own reality. Now he looks corrupted.

In every human encounter you will see it happening—people are throwing their authority all around; either bullying people or being bullied by others. And if somebody bullies you, you will immediately find some weaker person somewhere to take the revenge.

If your boss bullies you in the office, you will come home and bully your wife. And if she is not a feminist, then she will wait for the child to come home from the school, and she will bully the child. And if the child is old-fashioned, not American, then the child will go to his room and crush his toys, because that is the only thing he can bully. He can show his power on the toy. But this goes on and on. This seems to be the whole game. This is what real politics is.

So whenever you have some authority. . . . And everybody has some authority or other. You cannot find a person, you cannot find the last person who has no authority; even he has some authority, even he has a dog he can kick. Everybody has some authority somewhere. So, everybody lives in politics. You may not be a member of any political party; that doesn't mean that you are not political. If you abuse your authority, you are political. If you don't abuse your authority, then you are non-political.

Become more aware not to abuse your authority. It will give a new light to how you function and it will make you so calm and centered. It will give you tranquility and serenity.

8 of Clouds: Guilt

The word guilt should never be used. The very word has wrong associations; and once you use it you are caught in it.

The concept of sin is a technique of creating guilt in people.

You will have to understand the whole strategy of sin and guilt. Unless you make a person feel guilty, you cannot enslave him psychologically. It is impossible to imprison him in a certain ideology, a certain belief system. But once you have created guilt in his mind, you have taken all that is courageous in him. You have destroyed all that is adventurous in him. You have repressed all possibility of his ever being an individual in his own right. With the idea of guilt, you have almost murdered the human potential in him. He can never be independent. The guilt will force him to be dependent on a messiah, on a religious teaching, on God, on the concepts of heaven and hell and the whole lot.

To create guilt, all that you need is a very simple thing: start calling mistakes and errors "sins." They are simply mistakes, human. Now, if somebody commits a mistake in mathematics—two plus two, and he concludes it makes five—you don't say he has committed a sin. He is unalert, he is not paying attention to what he is doing. He is unprepared, he has not done his homework. He is certainly committing a mistake, but a mistake is not a sin. It can be corrected. A mistake does not make him feel guilty. At the most it makes him feel foolish.

Guilt is an idea accepted by you. You can reject it, and it can be rejected because it is not part of existence.

Guilt is not a natural phenomenon, it is created by the priests. Through guilt they have exploited humanity. The whole history of pseudo-religion is contained in the word *guilt*—it is the most poisoned word. Beware of it; never use it, because in your unconscious mind it also has deep roots. You cannot find guilt in any animal; the animal simply is. It has no ideals, it has no arts; it exists, and simply exists. It has no perfections to be attained and hence the animal is beautiful, innocent.

Ideals corrupt. Once you have an ideal to fulfill you will never be at ease, and you will never be at home, and you can never be contented. Dissatisfaction follows ideals like a shadow, and the more dissatisfied you are with yourself, the more it becomes impossible to reach the ideal: this is the vicious circle. If you are not dissatisfied with yourself, if you accept yourself as you are, the ideal can be fulfilled immediately. And I emphasize the word *immediately*—with no time gap, right this moment, here and now, you can realize that you are perfect; it is not something to be attained in the future, it is something that you have always been carrying within you. Perfection is your nature—perfect you are.

I am against guilt—the guilt that has been created by the priests—but there is a different type of guilt which is not created by the priest. And that guilt is very meaningful. That guilt arises if you feel there is something more in life and you are not working hard to get to it. Then you feel guilt. Then you feel that somehow you are creating barriers to your own growth—that you are lazy, lethargic, unconscious, asleep; that you don't have any integration, that you cannot move towards your destiny. Then a kind of guilt arises. When you feel that you have the possibility and you are not turning it into actuality, then guilt arises. That guilt is totally different.

There is a real spiritual guilt, which has nothing to do with any politics, with any priesthood, with any religion or church. That guilt feeling is very natural. When you see that you can do something and you are not doing it, when you see your potential but you are not changing that potential into actuality . . . when you see that you are carrying tremendous treasures as seeds which could bloom, and you are not doing anything about it and you are just remaining in misery—then you feel a great responsibility towards yourself. And if you are not fulfilling that responsibility, you feel guilty. This guilt is of tremendous import.

9 of Clouds: Sorrow

Bliss has not to be found outside, against sorrow. Bliss has to be found deep, hidden behind the sorrow itself. You have to dig into your sorrowful states and you will find a wellspring of joy.

You are sad. Go into your sadness rather than escaping into some activity, into some occupation. Rather than going to see a friend or to a movie or turning on the radio or the TV, rather than escaping from it, turning your back to it, drop all activity. Close your eyes, go into it, see what it is, why it is—and see without condemning it, because if you condemn you will not be able to see the totality of it. See without judging. If you judge, you will not be able to see the whole of it. Without judgment, without condemnation, without evaluation, just watch it, watch what it is. Look at it as if it is a flower, sad; a cloud, dark; but look at it with no judgment so that you can see all the facets of it.

And you will be surprised: the deeper you go into it, the more it starts dispersing. If a person can go into his sorrow deeply he will find all sorrow has evaporated. In that evaporation of sorrow is joy, is bliss.

There are two types of sadness. One is causal: you have lost a friend and you are sorrowful, somebody has died and you are sorrowful— but time will heal that. It has a cause, and anything caused cannot be permanent. You will find another friend, you will have another lover, and you will forget about it. Only time is needed and it will be healed. But there is existential sorrow that has no cause. It persists, there is no reason for it; it is simply there as part of your growth.

You have become aware of the meaninglessness of life. You go on doing things but you have become capable of seeing through them. You know that it is pointless, hence the sorrow. You know that it's okay, it keeps one occupied, but it is just okay, nothing much; it is an occupation. You are no longer in deep illusion; hence the sorrow.

You are disillusioned. You have seen through things about which you had hopes, but now you can see that all hopes are baseless, that nothing is going to happen, that one can go on hoping and one day one dies. And everything fails—money fails, relationship fails, friendship fails, everything, sooner or later. Everything comes to a dead end, to a cul-de-sac, and then one is stuck. Just somehow, to go on, one drags oneself and starts doing something else. One has to do something, otherwise life will be too much of a burden, so one keeps oneself occupied. But one knows deep down that all is futile, that it is a tale told by an idiot.

When this happens it is beautiful. It is the beginning of transformation. You are a disillusioned being, and only a disillusioned being can search. When the world has no hope for you, you can go inward— when the outside has failed utterly . . . and I say utterly! Even if a slight hope is there, you will go on searching; then some illusion remains.

When you are utterly disillusioned, when the outer has no more attraction, when you have seen it and found it lacking and now you have come to the point of realizing that there is nothing—then the quantum leap into the inner.

10 of Clouds: Rebirth

The real sage again becomes a child. The circle is complete—from the child back to the child. But the difference is great. . . . The first birth is of the body and the second birth is of the consciousness.

Zarathustra divides the evolution of consciousness into three symbols: the camel, the lion, and the child. The camel is a beast of burden, ready to be enslaved, never rebellious. He cannot ever say no. He is a believer, a follower, a faithful slave. That is the lowest in human consciousness.

The lion is a revolution. The beginning of the revolution is a sacred no. In the consciousness of the camel there is always a need for someone to lead and someone to say to him, "Thou shalt do this." He needs the Ten Commandments. He needs all the religions, all the priests, and all the holy scriptures because he cannot trust himself. He has no courage and no soul and no longing for freedom. He's obedient.

The lion is a longing for freedom, a desire to destroy all imprisonments. The lion is not in need of any leader; he is enough unto himself. He will not allow anybody else to say to him, "Thou shalt." That is insulting to his pride. He can only say, "I will." The lion is responsibility and a tremendous effort to get out of all chains.

But even the lion is not the highest peak of human growth. The highest peak is when the lion also goes through a metamorphosis and becomes a child. The child is innocence. It is not obedience, it is not disobedience; it is not belief, it is not disbelief—it is pure trust, it is a sacred yes to existence and to life and to all that it contains. The child is the very peak of purity, sincerity, authenticity, receptivity, and openness to existence. These symbols are very beautiful.

Zarathustra is not in favor of the weak, in favor of the so-called humble. He is not in agreement with Jesus that "Blessed are the meek," that "Blessed are the poor," that "Blessed are the humble for they shall inherit the kingdom of God." Zarathustra is absolutely in favor of a strong spirit. He is against the ego, but he is not against pride. Pride is the dignity of man. Ego is a false entity and one should never think of them as synonymous.

The ego is something that deprives you of your dignity, that deprives you of your pride, because the ego has to depend on others, on the opinion of others, on what people say. The ego is very fragile. The opinion of people can change and the ego will disappear into the air.

Ego is a by-product of public opinion. They give it to you; they can take it away. Pride is a totally different phenomenon. The lion has pride. The deer in the forest—just look—has a pride, a dignity, grace. A peacock dancing or an eagle flying far away in the sky—they don't have egos, they don't depend on your opinion—they are simply digni-fied as they are. Their dignity arises from their own being. This has to be understood, because all the religions have been teaching people not to be proud—be humble. They have created a misunderstanding all over the world, as if being proud and being an egoist are synonymous.

Zarathustra is absolutely clear that he is in favor of the strong, of the courageous, of the adventurer who goes into the unknown on the untrodden path without any fear; he is in favor of fearlessness. And it is a miracle that a person of pride, and only a person of pride, can become a child.

The so-called Christian humbleness is just ego standing on its head. The ego has gone upside-down but it is there, and you can see in your saints that they are more egoistic than ordinary people are. They are egoists because of their piousness, their austerities, their spirituality, their holiness, even because of their humbleness. Nobody is more humble than they are. The ego has a very subtle way of coming in from the back door. You may throw it out from the front door—it knows that there is a back door too.

To choose the camel as the lowest consciousness is perfectly right.

The lowest consciousness in man is crippled; it wants to be enslaved. It is afraid of freedom because it is afraid of responsibility. It is ready to be loaded with as much burden as possible. It rejoices in being loaded; so does the lowest consciousness—being loaded with knowledge, which is borrowed. No man of dignity will allow himself to be loaded with borrowed knowledge. It is loaded with morality that has been handed over by the dead to the living; it is a domination of the dead over the living. No man of dignity will allow the dead to rule him.

The lowest consciousness of man remains ignorant and unconscious, unaware, fast asleep—because it is continuously being given the poison of believing, of faith, of never doubting, of never saying no. And a man who cannot say no has lost his dignity. A man who cannot say no . . . his yes does not mean anything. Do you see the implication? The yes is meaningful only after you are capable of saying no. If you are incapable of saying no, your yes is impotent; it means nothing.

Hence, the camel has to change into a beautiful lion, ready to die but not ready to be enslaved. You cannot make a lion a beast of burden. A lion has a dignity that no other animal can claim; he has no treasures, no kingdoms; his dignity is just in his style of being—fearless, unafraid of the unknown, ready to say no even at the risk of death.

This readiness to say no, this rebelliousness, cleans him of all the dirt that the camel has left—all the traces and the footprints that the camel has left. And only after the lion—after the great no—the sacred yes of a child is possible.

The child says yes not because he is afraid. He says yes because he loves, because he trusts. He says yes because he is innocent; he cannot conceive that he can be deceived. His yes is a tremendous trust. It is not out of fear, it is out of deep innocence. Only this yes can lead him to the ultimate peak of consciousness; what I call godliness.

The child is the highest peak of evolution as far as consciousness is concerned. But the child is only a symbol; it does not mean that children are the highest state of being. A child is used symbolically because it is not knowledgeable. It is innocent, and because it is innocent it is full of wonder, and because its eyes are full of wonder, its soul longs for the mysterious. A child is a beginning, a sport; and life should be always a beginning and always a playfulness; always a laughter and never seriousness.

A sacred yes is needed, but the sacred yes can come only after a sacred no. The camel also says yes but it is the yes of a slave. He cannot say no. His yes is meaningless.

The lion says no! But he cannot say yes. It is against his very nature. It reminds him of the camel. Somehow he has freed himself from the camel and to say yes naturally reminds him again—the yes of the camel and the slavery. No, the animal in the camel is incapable of saying no. In the lion, it is capable of saying no but is incapable of saying yes.

The child knows nothing of the camel, knows nothing of the lion. That's why Zarathustra says: "A child is innocence and forgetfulness. . . ." His yes is pure and he has every potential to say no. If he does not say it, it is because he trusts, not because he is afraid; not out of fear, but out of trust. And when yes comes out of trust, it is the greatest metamorphosis, the greatest transformation that one can hope for.

THE SUIT OF RAINBOWS
(DISKS, PENTACLES)

Reality—Ordinariness—Earth & Sky

A tree is more alive than any temple, than any church; a river is more alive than any mosque. The stone idols in your temples are dead; a tree is more alive. You may be superstitious, but the person who is worshipping a tree is not. He may not be aware of what he is doing, but a deep reverence for life in all its forms is there, a deep respect.

Wherever you feel that life is growing, celebrate it, love it, welcome it, and a great transformation will happen to you. If life is revered in all its forms, you become more alive.

Reality

Ordinarily, whatsoever we have become accustomed to know is just a mind game, because we look at that which is with loaded eyes. Our mirrors are covered with much dust; they have become incapable of reflecting the real. The real is not far away, the real surrounds you. You are part of it, it is part of you. You are not separate from it, you have never been separate from it. You cannot be separate from it— there is no way to be separate from it, it is impossible to be separate from it. But still, the dust-covered mirror is incapable of reflecting it.

Once the dust disappears, you will be surprised that all that you have been seeking need not be sought at all, because you have it already.

The spiritual search is as illusory as any other search. The search itself is illusory because it has taken one thing for granted: that something is missing. And nothing is missing! Once you take it for granted that something is missing you start looking for it; then you go on looking for it in all directions. And the more you search the more you will miss it, because the more you search the more dust-covered the mirror becomes. The more you travel to seek it, the farther and farther you go in search of it, the more and more frustrated you become. Slowly, slowly you start thinking that it is so far away. . . . "That's why I am not reaching it."

The reality is just the opposite: you are not reaching it because you are it. It is not far away, it is so close by that even to call it "close" is not right, because even closeness is a kind of distance. It is not distant at all, it breathes in you. It is not *there*, it is *here*. It is not *then*, it is *now*. It has always been with you. From the very beginning everyone is a buddha, everyone is a mirror capable of reflecting.

This is the basic message of Zen—and the greatest message that has ever been delivered to humanity, the most liberating force that has ever been brought to the earth. But you will have to look in a totally new way. All that is needed is not a search but a new way of looking at things. The common, the ordinary, the usual way has to be dropped.

Ordinariness

Zen is just Zen. There is nothing comparable to it. It is unique— unique in the sense that it is the most ordinary and yet the most extraordinary phenomenon that has happened to human consciousness. It is the most ordinary because it does not believe in knowledge, it does not believe in mind. It is not a philosophy, not a religion either. It is the acceptance of the ordinary existence with a total heart, with one's total being, not desiring some other world, supra-mundane, supra-mental. It has no interest in any esoteric nonsense, no interest in metaphysics at all. It does not hanker for the other shore; this shore is more than enough. Its acceptance of this shore is so tremendous that through that very acceptance it transforms this shore—and this very shore becomes the other shore:

This very body the buddha;
This very earth the lotus paradise.

Hence it is ordinary. It does not want you to create a certain kind of spirituality, a certain kind of holiness. All that it asks is that you live your life with immediacy, spontaneity. And then the mundane becomes the sacred.

The great miracle of Zen is in the transformation of the mundane into the sacred. And it is tremendously extraordinary because *this* way life has never been approached before; this way life has never been respected before.

Zen goes beyond Buddha and beyond Lao Tzu. It is a culmination, a transcendence, both of the Indian genius and of the Chinese genius. The Indian genius reached its highest peak in Gautam the Buddha and the Chinese genius reached its highest peak in Lao Tzu. And the essence of Buddha's teaching and the essence of Lao Tzu's teaching merged into one stream so deeply that no separation is possible now. Even to make a distinction between what belongs to Buddha and what to Lao Tzu is impossible, the merger has been so total. It is not only a synthesis, it is an integration. Out of this meeting Zen was born. Zen is neither Buddhist nor Taoist and yet both.

To call Zen "Zen Buddhism" is not right because it is far more. Buddha is not so earthly as Zen is. Lao Tzu is tremendously earthly, but Zen is not only earthly: its vision transforms the earth into heaven. Lao Tzu is earthly, Buddha is unearthly, Zen is both—and in being both it has become the most extraordinary phenomenon.

Earth & Sky

The future of humanity will go closer and closer to the approach of Zen, because the meeting of the East and West is possible only through something which is earthly and yet unearthly. The West is very earthly, the East is very unearthly. Who is going to become the bridge? Buddha cannot be the bridge; he is so essentially Eastern, the very flavor of the East, the very fragrance of the East, uncompromising. Lao Tzu cannot be the bridge; he is too earthly. China has always been very earthly. China is more part of the Western psyche than of the Eastern psyche.

It is not an accident that China was the first country in the East to turn communist, to become materialist, to believe in a godless philosophy, to believe that man is only matter and nothing else. This is not just accidental. China has been earthly for almost five thousand years; it is very Western. Hence Lao Tzu cannot become the bridge; he is more like Zorba the Greek. Buddha is so unearthly you cannot even catch hold of him—how can he become the bridge?

When I look all around, Zen seems to be the only possibility, because in Zen, Buddha and Lao Tzu have become one. The meeting has already happened. The seed is there, the seed of that great bridge that can make East and West one. Zen is going to be the meeting point. It has a great future—a great past and a great future.

And the miracle is that Zen is neither interested in the past nor in the future. Its total interest is in the present. Maybe that's why the miracle is possible, because the past and the future are bridged by the present.

The present is not part of time. Have you ever thought about it? How long is the present? The past has a duration, the future has a duration. What is the duration of the present? How long does it last? Between the past and the future, can you measure the present? It is immeasurable; it is almost not. It is not time at all: it is the penetration of eternity into time.

And Zen lives in the present. The whole teaching is how to be in the present—how to get out of the past which is no more, and how not to get involved in the future which is not yet, and just to be rooted, centered, in that which is.

The whole approach of Zen is of immediacy, but because of that it can bridge the past and the future. It can bridge many things: it can bridge the past and the future, it can bridge the East and the West, it can bridge body and soul. It can bridge the unbridgeable worlds: this world and that, the mundane and the sacred.

King of Rainbows: Abundance

One thing is certain: Existence is overflowing. With everything it is luxurious. It is not a poor existence, no. Poverty is man's creation.

Life means abundance, richness, in every possible dimension. Just look at existence. Do you think it is poor? Look at the millions of flowers, their fragrance; look at the millions of stars. Man has not been able yet to count them, and I don't think he is ever going to be able to count them. With your bare, naked eye you only see, at the most, three thousand stars—and that's nothing. And these stars are expanding. Just as a flower opens up and the petals start going away from the center, the universe is continuously flowering, blossoming, opening—and with a tremendous speed. The stars are going farther away from the center. We don't know exactly where the center is; but one thing is certain, that the whole universe is running fast, moving, alive.

Most people don't know what life is for. They have never lived. Yes, they have been born; but just to be born is not enough to be alive. They will vegetate and think they are living. And one day they will die, without ever having lived at all. These are the miracles that go on happening all around the world; people who have never lived, die—such an impossibility! But it happens every day. And many have recognized it at the moment of death, and have said it is so: "It is strange; for the first time I am realizing that I missed life."

If you live, for what? To love, to enjoy, to be ecstatic—otherwise why live at all?

And what is richness? Just making life more and more enjoyable, more and more lovable, more and more comfortable, more and more luxurious.

The man who knows nothing of the great world of music is poor; he is missing one of the greatest luxuries of life. The man who does not know how to enjoy Picasso, van Gogh, does not know anything about the colors. If he cannot enjoy Leonardo da Vinci, how can he enjoy a sunrise, a sunset? Millions of people go on living, never recognizing a sunrise, never stopping for a moment to look at a sunset and all the colors that the sunset leaves behind in the sky. Millions of people never raise their eyes towards the sky and the splendor of it.

Living can only mean one thing: living life multi-dimensionally— the music, the poetry, the painting, the sculpture . . . but it is all luxury.

Queen of Rainbows: Flowering

This world needs only one experience: a purity, uncontaminated, unpolluted even by the presence of anybody else. A pure presence of your own being—to me, that is the liberation. To me, that is the ultimate flowering of your being.

The moment spring comes all the trees rejoice, they welcome the spring with their flowers, with their perfume. In the East, orange is the color of spring. Its Hindi name is *vasanti*; it is from *vasant*—spring. It is the color of the flowers.

There are wildflowers that explode in the springtime and the whole forest seems to be afire. It suddenly becomes covered with flowers and flowers; you cannot even see the leaves.

Bliss also functions in the same way for your inner flowering, for the flowers of your consciousness. So don't be serious. Seriousness is a disease that has to be avoided. You are not to be sad; you have to be cheerful, enjoying small things of life, not bothering about whether these things are worth enjoying or not. The real thing is to enjoy; what you are enjoying is immaterial.

If you can enjoy even ordinary things of life, of course you will become capable of enjoying the extraordinary. And the person who cannot enjoy the ordinary lacks the capacity to enjoy anything.

Omar Khayyam was a Sufi master who has been very much misunderstood because Fitzgerald, who translated him for the first time into English, could not understand the Sufi message. His translation is the best possible, and as a poet he has done something superb—many translations have been done of the *Rubaiyat of Omar Khayyam* but nothing has gone beyond the translation of Fitzgerald—but he was not a mystic, just a poet. So he understood the language, the beauty of the language, he translated it very sincerely, but still he missed the point and created a misunderstanding around the world about Omar Khayyam.

People started thinking that Omar Khayyam was just a drunkard—talking about wine, song, and dance—that he was just a materialist, that "Eat, drink, and be merry" was his message. This is a great misunderstanding and very unjust to Omar Khayyam.

Wine, song, and dance are symbols. What he means by using them is that one should enjoy even small things—eating, drinking—just the small things of life, things of no spiritual quality. But the spiritual quality comes from your enjoyment, not from the things. One can eat just ordinary food with such joy, with such gratitude, with such prayer, that it becomes a meditation. It starts having the quality of the sacred.

In one of his poems Omar Khayyam says, "I want to warn the so-called saints that if they don't enjoy this life they will become incapable of enjoying the other." And he is perfectly right, because enjoying something is an art and this life is an opportunity to learn the art.

If you cannot enjoy flowers here how will you be able to enjoy flowers in paradise?

Those flowers may be of gold, studded with diamonds—everlasting, eternal—but if you cannot enjoy the momentary, not even the momentary, how will you enjoy the eternal? The momentary gives you an opportunity to learn the art—that's the whole function of life.

So you have to enjoy everything possible. Go on finding ways to enjoy even things which seem on the surface unenjoyable. If you search you will find some way to enjoy even the unenjoyable things. And that's the whole process of inner transformation. A moment comes when you can enjoy everything. That is the moment when light descends, when existence penetrates you—you are ready, your heart is ready.

Knight of Rainbows: Slowing Down

Slow down all the processes that you do. If you are walking, walk slowly—there is no hurry. If you are eating, eat slowly. If you are talking, talk slowly.

Slow down all the processes, and you will see that you can become silent very easily.

Hurry is killing many people. People are hurrying for no reason at all, there is nowhere to go, but they are hurrying. They go on becoming more and more speedy. Nobody is bothered about where you are going and why you are going at such a speed. Speed seems to be, in itself, the goal. If somebody comes with any idea that the speed can be increased, people are ready to take it immediately.

There is a very old story, a Taoist story. A man had invented some machine to draw water from the well. He came into a garden to see an old man—very old, ancient—with his young boy. Both were pulling the water out, and it was hard and the old man was perspiring.

The man said, "Have not you heard about mechanical devices? Now there is no need!"

The old man said, "Keep quiet! When my boy is gone then I will talk to you."

When the boy had gone to eat, the old man said, "Don't talk nonsense here. If he hears this, he is yet too young, and he may be corrupted by it."

The man said, "What are you saying? Are you in your senses? I am saying that you can save much labor."

But the old man said, "What is one going to do with that labor then? For what? I am one hundred years old and I am still alive enough to do all my work. If I had depended on mechanical devices, I would be dead by now. My young boy is very young—please don't say such things before him, otherwise he may get your ideas, may become interested. Young people are foolish!"

And this is not just a story. In fact the first beginnings of all the great inventions that are the fundamentals of all scientific progress were done in the East—in China and India. But India and China never developed them, knowing well that speed and efficiency only create more worry, make people tense . . . and time is not saved! Even if time is saved, what is one going to do with that time? You will worry in that time.

First you have the time, and then you worry and become anxious and ask for some entertainment, because now what to do with the time? First you save time, and then you ask how to kill time. So there are people who sell ideas for how to become speedier and more effi-cient; then there are people who go on selling ideas for how to enter-tain yourself when time is there. It is just absurd!

So try one thing—slow down. And just by slowing down ordinary processes, you will see how peaceful you can become. Eat slowly—take time! If you eat in twenty minutes, why not in forty? There is no hurry! Enjoy the food! Chew it more; it will be digested better. Your body will feel more at ease and at home. And of course when the body is at home, the mind too feels at home.

Sometimes when you don't have anything to do, just sit silently doing nothing. There is no need to read the newspaper or to watch the TV. Don't be in such a mad rush to occupy yourself. That is a way to escape from oneself. So sometimes when you have nothing to do, feel happy that you have some time when you have nothing to do. Then just sit silently, look at the stars or at the trees, or just close your eyes and look inward.

If you can sit silently every day at least for one hour, within three, four months, you will know for the first time what peace is. And unless one has known what peace is, one has not known what life is. Only in a surfacing of peace, when the springs of peace start flowing in you, do you feel the meaning of life. Otherwise it is much ado about nothing.

Page of Rainbows: Adventure

Life is an adventure. Invite constant adventures, and whenever a call comes from the unknown, listen to it. Risk all and go into the unknown, because this is the only way to live at the maximum.

Life is a great adventure, but people are so afraid that they cling to the familiar, to the known, to the well defined, to the logical. They never go beyond the boundary of the mind. If you live in the mind you are living in a grave. If you go beyond the mind you are really born, you have come out of the grave.

One can live each moment with such intensity, with such adventure, that each moment becomes a great gift because it brings so much joy, so much ecstasy. But one has to be ready to go on dropping the past. One should not allow the past to be accumulated. That becomes a prison wall around you. Each moment die to the past and remain fresh, and your life will be a great adventure. And it is only for the adventurous people to know what truth is. The non-adventurous live in comfortable lies.

Skill has something in it, and that is security. It misses something, and that is adventure. So all secure lives will be non-adventurous and all adventurous lives will be insecure.

If you are in a situation where you cannot have new friends every day, then use the beauty of old friendship as much as you can. If you are in a situation where friends change every day, that's perfectly good—you have the opportunity to make new friends, fresh friendships. And fresh friendships have a beauty of their own. Life is more alive, there is more adventure. To be friendly with a stranger is more adventurous, to trust the stranger is more adventurous and more dangerous, and to go on finding new persons to love and be friendly with will help you to flow more. Again and again they will be gone—by the time things are settling and you are feeling that now things are becoming secure, they are gone. But it is good!

Ordinarily we would like to have all the joy with all the security— and that doesn't happen. That's not the way of life, and nothing can be done about it. That's what we want: we want the impossible. We want security, safety, control, and we want joy, celebration, and great adventure. Both things cannot happen together, you cannot have both. They don't come in the same package.

Life is an adventure. Invite constant adventures, and whenever a call comes from the unknown, listen to it. Risk all and go into the unknown, because this is the only way to live at the maximum.

Ace of Rainbows: Maturity

Maturity has nothing to do with your life experiences.

It has something to do with your inward journey, experiences of the inner.

The more a person goes deeper into himself, the more mature he is. When he has reached the very center of his being, he is perfectly mature. But at that moment the person disappears, only presence remains. . . . The self disappears, only silence remains. Knowledge disappears, only innocence remains.

Maturity is another name for realization: you have come to the fulfillment of your potential, it has become actual. The seed has come on a long journey, and has blossomed.

Maturity has a fragrance. It gives a tremendous beauty to the individual. It gives intelligence, the sharpest possible intelligence. It makes him nothing but love. His action is love, his inaction is love; his life is love, his death is love. He is just a flower of love.

The West has definitions of maturity that are very childish. The West means by maturity that you are no longer innocent, that you have ripened through life experiences, that you cannot be cheated easily, that you cannot be exploited, that you have within you something like a solid rock—a protection, a security.

This definition is very ordinary, very worldly. Yes, in the world you will find mature people of this type. But the way I see maturity is totally different, diametrically opposite to this definition. The maturity will not make you a rock; it will make you so vulnerable, so soft, so simple.

Maturity to me is a spiritual phenomenon.

2 of Rainbows: Moment to Moment

MOMENT TO MOMENT

The mind cannot trust the moment; it is always afraid; that's why it plans.

It is fear that plans, and by planning you miss everything—everything that is beautiful and true, everything that is divine, you miss.

Life is such a flux, nothing remains the same, everything moves. Heraclitus has said that you cannot step twice in the same river—how can you plan? By the time you are stepping the second time, much water has flowed, it is not the same river. Planning is possible if the past repeats itself. But the past never repeats itself, repetition never happens—even if you see something repeating itself, it is just because you cannot see the whole.

Heraclitus again—he says, every day the sun is new. Of course you will say it is the same sun—but it cannot be the same, there is no possibility of its being the same. Much has changed; the whole sky is different, the whole pattern of stars is different, the sun itself has become older. Now scientists say that within four million years the sun will die, its death is coming near—because the sun is an alive phenomenon and it is very old, it has to die.

Suns are born, they live—and they die. Four million years for us is very long; for the sun it is just nothing, it is as if the next moment it is going to die. And when the sun dies, the whole solar family will disappear, because the sun is the source. Every day the sun is dying, and becoming older and older and older—it cannot be the same. Every day energy is lost—a vast amount of energy is being thrown off in the sunrays. The sun is less every day, becoming exhausted. It is not the same, it cannot be the same.

And when the sun rises, it rises upon a different world, and the onlooker also is not the same. Yesterday you may have been filled with love; then your eyes were different, and the sun of course looked different. You were so filled with love that a certain quality of poetry was around you, and you looked through that poetry—the sun may have looked like a god, as it looked to the seers of the Vedas. They called the sun "God"—they must have been filled with so much poetry. They were poets, in love with existence; they were not scientists. They were not in search of what matter was, they were in search of what the mood was. They worshipped the sun. They must have been very happy and blissful people, because you can worship only when you feel a blessing; you can worship only when you feel that your whole life is a blessing.

Yesterday you may have been a poet, today you may not be a poet at all—because every moment the river is flowing within you. You are also changing. Yesterday things were fitting into each other, today everything is a mess: you are angry, you are depressed, you are sad. How can the sun be the same when the onlooker has changed? Everything changes, so a man of understanding never exactly plans for the future, cannot—but he is more ready than you to meet the future. This is the paradox. You plan, but you are not so ready.

In fact, planning means that you feel so inadequate, that's why you plan—otherwise, why plan? A guest is coming, and you plan what you are going to say to him. What nonsense! When the guest comes, can't you be spontaneous? But you are afraid, you don't believe in yourself, you have no trust; you plan, you go through a rehearsal. Your life is an acting, it is not a real thing, because a rehearsal is needed only in acting. And remember: when you have gone through a rehearsal, whatsoever happens will be an act, not the real thing.

The guest has not arrived and you are planning already what you will say, how you will greet him, how you are going to respond. You are already saying things. The guest, in the mind, has already arrived—you are talking to him.

In fact, by the time the guest arrives you will be fed up with him. In fact, by the time the guest arrives he has already been with you too long—you are bored, and whatsoever you say will not be true and authentic. It will not come from you, it will come from the memory. It will not pop up from your existence, it will come from the rehearsal that you have been having. It will be false—and a meeting will not be possible, because how can a false man meet? And it may be the same with your guest: he was also planning, he also is fed up with you already. He has talked too much and now he would like to be silent, and whatsoever he says will be out of the rehearsal.

So wherever two persons meet, there are four persons meeting—at least; more are possible. Two real ones are in the background, two false ones meeting each other and encountering. Everything is false, because it comes out of planning. Even when you love a person you plan, and go through a rehearsal—all the movements that you are going to make, how you are going to kiss, the gestures—and everything becomes false. Why don't you trust yourself? When the moment comes, why don't you trust your spontaneity? Why can't you be real?

The mind cannot trust the moment; it is always afraid, that's why it plans. Planning means fear. It is fear that plans, and by planning you miss everything—everything that is beautiful and true, everything that is divine, you miss.

Millions of possibilities will be there. Don't fix it beforehand. Just be aware and alert and let things happen.

3 of Rainbows: Guidance

We have lost contact with the inner guide.
Everyone is born with that inner guide but it is not allowed to work, to function. It is almost paralyzed. But it can be revived.

Zen Masters teach swordsmanship as a meditation and they say, "Be moment to moment with the inner guide, don't think. Allow the inner being to do whatsoever happens to it. Don't interfere with the mind."

This is very difficult because we are so trained with our minds. Our schools, our colleges, our universities, the whole culture, the whole pattern of civilization, teach our heads. We have lost contact with the inner guide. Everyone is born with that inner guide but it is not allowed to work, to function. It is almost paralyzed, but it can be revived.

Don't think with the head. Really, don't think at all. Just move. Try it in some situations. It will be difficult, because the old habit will be to start thinking. You will have to be alert: not to think, but to feel inwardly what is coming to the mind. You may be confused many times because you will not be able to know whether it is coming from the inner guide or from the surface of the mind. But soon you will know the feeling, the difference.

When something comes from the inner, it comes from your navel upwards. You can feel the flow, the warmth, coming from the navel upwards. Whenever your mind thinks, it is just on the surface, in the head, and then it goes down. If your mind decided something, then you have to force it down. If your inner guide decides, then something bubbles up in you. It comes from the deep core of your being towards the mind. The mind receives it, but it is not of the mind. It comes from beyond—and that is why the mind is scared about it. For the reason it is not reliable because it comes from behind—without any proofs. It simply bubbles up.

Try it in certain situations. For example, you have lost your path in a forest. Try it. Don't think—just close your eyes, sit down, be meditative, and don't think. Because it is futile—how can you think? You don't know. But thinking has become such a habit that you go on thinking even in moments when nothing can come out of it. Thinking can think only about something that is already known. You are lost in a forest, you don't have any map, there is nobody you can ask. What are you thinking about? But still you think. That thinking will be just a worry, not a thinking. And the more you get worried, the less the inner guide can be competent.

Be unworried. Sit down under a tree, and just allow thoughts to drop and subside. Just wait, don't think. Don't create a problem, just wait. And when you feel a moment of non-thinking has come, then stand up and start moving. Wherever your body moves, allow it to move. You just be a witness. Don't interfere. The lost path can be found very easily. But the only condition is, don't interfere with the mind.

This has happened many times unknowingly. Great scientists say that whenever a great discovery has been made, it was never made by the mind; it was always made by the inner guide.

Madame Curie was trying and trying to solve a mathematical problem. She did her best, all that was possible. Then she got fed up. For days together, weeks together, she had been working and nothing had come out. She was feeling just mad. No path was leading to the solution. Then one night, just exhausted, she fell down and slept. And in the night, in a dream, the conclusion bubbled up. She was so concerned with the conclusion that the dream was broken, she awoke. Immediately she wrote down the conclusion—because there was no process in the dream, just a conclusion. She wrote it down on a pad and then slept again. In the morning she was puzzled; the conclusion was right, but she didn't know how it had been achieved. There was no process, no method. Then she tried to find the process; now it was an easier affair because the conclusion was in the hand, and it is easy to go back from the conclusion. She won the Nobel Prize because of this dream—but she always wondered how it happened.

When your mind gets exhausted and cannot do any more, it simply retires. In that moment of retirement the inner guide can give hints, clues, keys. The man who won the Nobel Prize for the inner structure of a human cell, saw it in a dream. He saw the whole structure of the human cell, the inner cell, in a dream, and then in the morning he just made a picture of it. He himself couldn't believe that it could be so, so he had to work for years. After years of work he could conclude that the dream was true.

With Madame Curie it happened that when she came to know this inner process of the inner guide, she decided to try it. Once there was a problem which she wanted to solve, so she thought, "Why worry about it, and why try? Just go to sleep." She slept well, but there was no solution. So she was puzzled. Many times she tried: when there was a problem immediately she would go to sleep. But there was no solution. First, the intellect has to be tried completely; only then can the solution bubble up. The head has to be completely exhausted otherwise it goes on functioning, even in a dream.

So now scientists say that all the great discoveries are intuitive, not intellectual. This is what is meant by the inner guide.

Lose the head and drop into this inner guide. It is there.

4 of Rainbows: The Miser

Generosity is the real richness.

The poor are always generous, the rich never. That's how they become rich. If a rich man is generous, a revolution has happened. A rich man becomes generous only when he has attained to a deep understanding that riches are useless. When he has come to know that all that this world can give is not worth taking, only then does generosity become possible— then he starts sharing.

Otherwise, you go on accumulating more and more and more. The mind goes on asking for more. There is no end to it. If you are not alert, all the riches of all the worlds will not be enough—because the mind does not bother what you have. It simply goes on saying "More!"

The mind goes on for more and more and more. It doesn't bother what you have. You may be a beggar—it asks for more; you may be an emperor—it asks for more. The nature of the mind is to ask for more. It is not relevant, what you have. It is the very nature of the mind just to go on asking for more. A rich man goes on asking for more, and remains poor. He goes on desiring for more, and remains poor. It is difficult to find a really rich man.

Generosity is the real richness.

And to be generous, to share, you don't need many things. To be generous, you just have to share whatsoever you have. You may not have much—that is not the point. Who has much? Who can ever have enough? It is never plenty, it is never enough. You may not have anything at all, you may be just a beggar on the road, but still you can be generous.

Can't you smile when a stranger passes by? You can smile, you can share your being with a stranger, and then you are generous. Can't you sing when somebody is sad? You can be generous—smiles cost nothing. But you have become so miserly that even before smiling you think thrice: to smile or not to smile? to sing or not to sing? to dance or not to dance?—in fact, to be or not to be?

Share your being if you have nothing. And that is the greatest wealth—everybody is born with it. Share your being! Stretch out your hand, move towards the other with love in the heart. Don't think anybody is a stranger. Nobody is. Or, everybody is. If you share, nobody is. If you don't share, everybody is.

You may be a very rich man but a miser, a non-sharing one. Then your own children are strangers, then your own wife is a stranger—because how can you really meet a miserly man? He is closed. He is already dead in his grave. How can you move towards a miserly man? If you move, he escapes. He is always afraid, because whenever somebody comes close, sharing starts. Even shaking hands a miserly man feels is dangerous, because who knows?—friendship may grow out of it, and then there is danger.

A miserly man is always alert, on guard, not to allow anybody too close. He keeps everybody at a distance. A smile is dangerous because it breaks distances. If you smile at a beggar on the road, the distance is bridged. He is no more a beggar, he has become a friend. Now, if he is hungry, you will have to do something. It is better to go on without smiling. It is safe, more economical, less dangerous—no risk in it.

It is not a question of sharing something. It is a question of simple sharing—whatsoever you have! If you don't have anything else, you have a warm body—you can sit close with somebody and give your warmth. You can smile, you can dance, you can sing; you can laugh, and help the other to laugh.

5 of Rainbows: The Outsider

THE OUTSIDER

The moment you enter to the center of your being, you are no longer an outsider.
For the first time you are the insider.

Everybody is an outsider; howsoever you pretend, you remain an outsider. Unless one enters into the whole, one remains an outsider. We pretend, we try to create a small oasis of relationship—friends, relatives, children, husband, wife—and we try to hide behind these things. But death comes and destroys all, and suddenly we are naked in our outsiderness.

No, in this world you cannot be an insider unless you have moved into the whole. This world belongs to the whole. Only by belonging to the whole do you become part of this existence—otherwise not. These trees will remain strangers to you and so will the birds and the sun and the moon and the sands and the rains. Everything will remain a stranger unless you have made a contact with the divine. With that contact the whole quality of life changes.

Not to belong is one of the greatest experiences of life. To be utterly an outsider, never feeling to be a part anywhere, is a great experience of transcendence.

An American tourist went to see a Sufi Master. For many years he had heard about him, had fallen in deep love with his words, his message. Finally he decided to go to see him. When he entered his room he was surprised—it was an utterly empty room! The Master was sitting; there was no furniture at all! The American could not conceive of a living space without any furniture. He immediately asked, "Where is your furniture, sir?"

And the old Sufi laughed and he said, "And where is yours?"

And the American said, "Of course I am a tourist here. I cannot go on carrying my furniture!"

And the old man said, "So am I a tourist for only just a few days, and then I will be gone, just as you will be gone."

This world is just a pilgrimage—of great significance, but not a place to belong to, not a place to become part of. To be an insider in this world is to get lost. The worldly is the insider; a buddha is bound to remain an outsider. All buddhas are outsiders. Even if they are in the crowd they are alone. Even if they are in the marketplace they are not there. Even if they relate they remain separate. There is a kind of subtle distance that is always there.

And that distance is freedom, that distance is great joy, that distance is your own space. Do you call yourself a loner? You must be comparing yourself with others: "They are having so many relationships, they are having love affairs. They belong to each other, they are insiders—and I am a loner. Why?" You must be creating anguish unnecessarily.

My approach always is: whatsoever existence has given to you must be a subtle necessity of your soul, otherwise it would not have been given in the first place.

Think more of aloneness. Celebrate aloneness, celebrate your pure space, and great song will arise in your heart. And it will be a song of awareness, it will be a song of meditation. It will be a song of an alone bird calling in the distance—not calling to somebody in particular, but just calling because the heart is full and wants to call, because the cloud is full and wants to rain, because the flower is full and the petals open and the fragrance is released . . . unaddressed. Let your aloneness become a dance.

6 of Rainbows: Compromise

COMPROMISE

Compromise is ugly. . . . How can truth compromise with lies?

Religions cannot exist without the devil. They need a God and they need a devil also. So do not be misguided if you see only a God in their temples. Just behind that God the devil is hiding, because no religion can exist without the devil.

Something has to be condemned, something has to be fought, something has to be destroyed. The total is not accepted, only part. This is very basic. You are not accepted totally by any religion, only partially. They say, "We accept your love, but not your hate. Destroy hate." And this is a very deep problem, because when you destroy hate completely love is also destroyed—because they are not two. They say, "We accept your silence, but we do not accept your anger." Destroy anger and your aliveness is destroyed. Then you will be silent, but not an alive man— only a dead one. That silence is not life, it is just death.

Religions always divide you into two: the evil and the divine. They accept the divine and are against the evil—the evil has to be destroyed. So if someone really follows them, he will come to conclude that the moment you destroy the devil, God is destroyed. But no one really follows them—no one can follow them because the very teaching is absurd. So what is everyone doing? Everyone is just deceiving. That is why there is so much hypocrisy. That hypocrisy has been created by religion. You cannot do whatsoever they are teaching you to do, so you become a hypocrite. If you follow them you will die; if you do not follow them you feel guilty that you are irreligious. So what to do?

The cunning mind makes a compromise. It goes on paying lip service to them, saying, "I am following you," but it goes on doing whatsoever it wants to do. You continue your anger, you continue your sex, you continue your greed, but you go on saying that greed is bad, anger is bad, sex is bad—it is a sin.

This is hypocrisy. The whole world has become hypocritical, nobody is honest. Unless these divisive religions disappear, nobody can be honest. This will look contradictory because all the religions are teaching to be honest, but they are the foundation stones of all dishonesty. They make you dishonest; because they teach you to do impossible things, which you cannot do, you become hypocrites.

You have to create your own path to your own temple. No help is possible, and it is the grandeur of humanity, a tremendous dignity, that you can follow only your own path.

All religions are leading people wrongly; they are destroying people, making them into sheep. An authentic religion will make a man into a lion who walks alone, who never walks in a crowd. The crowd never suits him, because with the crowd you have always to compromise. With the crowd you have always to listen to others: their criticism, their appraisal, their conceptions of right and wrong, their values of good and bad.

In the crowd you cannot remain natural. The crowd is a very unnatural environment. Unless you are very aware, the crowd is going to crush you into dust. It is because of this that you don't find many buddhas in the world. A buddha has to fight inch by inch for his individuality. He has not to give way to the crowd, whatever the cost. Unless such an uncompromising attitude remains constantly in you, you cannot remain unaffected by the crowd in which you live.

And unfortunately everybody is born in a crowd—the parents, the teachers, the neighbors. Nobody is fortunate enough to be born alone, so that is out of the question. You are born in the society, in the crowd. Unless you can keep your intelligence clean of the pollution that will be surrounding you from every side, sooner or later you will become somebody else, somebody who nature had never intended you to be.

Remember constantly that you have your own destiny, just as everybody else has his own destiny. Unless you become the flower, the seeds of which you have been carrying within you, you will not feel blissfulness, fulfillment, contentment, you will not be able to dance in the wind, in the rain, in the sun. You can be in paradise only as an individual, if you have followed the path that you create by walking. There are no ready-made pathways.

When you enter in, you enter into pure space—not a road; there are not even footprints. Buddha used to say that the inner world is just like the sky. The birds fly but they don't leave their footprints. Nobody can follow their footprints because in the sky their footprints are not; as they have flown away, their footprints have dissolved.

The inner sky remains always pure, just waiting for you, because nobody can get inside you.

7 of Rainbows: Patience

When people start working towards the inner, impatience is the greatest barrier. Infinite patience is needed. It can happen the next moment, but infinite patience is needed.

There is one Zen saying which says, "Hurry slowly." That's right! Hurry, that's right, because you are going to die—in that sense hurry. But inside, if you are in too much of a hurry, you will miss, because you will conclude too soon, before your eyes have become attuned. Don't conclude too soon.

Hurry slowly. Just wait! Go there and sit and wait. By and by, a new world of the invisible becomes clear, comes to you. You become attuned to it, then you can hear the harmony, the melody; the silence starts its own music. It is always there, but it is so silent that very trained ears are needed. It is not like a noise, it is like silence. The sound within is like silence, the form within is like the formless. There is no time and no space within, and all that you know is either in space or in time. Things are in space, events are in time, and now physicists say these two things are not two; even time is just a fourth dimension of space.

You know only time and space, the world of things and events. You don't know the world of the witnessing self. It is beyond both, it is not confined to any space and it is not confined to any time. There is duration without time, there is space but without any height, length, breadth—it is a totally different world. You will need to become attuned to it, so don't be impatient—impatience is the greatest barrier. I have come to feel that when people start working towards the inner, impatience is the greatest barrier. Infinite patience is needed. It can happen the next moment, but infinite patience is needed.

If you are impatient it may not happen for lives, because the very impatience will not allow you the repose that Jesus talks about, the tranquillity. Even if you are expecting, that will be a disturbance. If you are thinking something is going to happen, something extraordinary, then nothing will happen. If you are waiting, expecting that some enlightenment is going to happen, you will miss it. Don't expect. All expectations belong to the world of death, the dimension of time and space.

No goal belongs to the inner. There is no way to it except by waiting, infinite patience. Jesus has said, "Watch and be patient." And one day, suddenly you are illumined. One day, when the right tuning happens, when you are ready, suddenly you are illumined. All darkness disappears, you are filled with life, eternal life, which never dies.

Patience is very alert, patience is very active, patience is very expectant. If you are waiting for somebody—a friend is to call—you may be sitting just by the door, but you are very attentive, alert. Any noise on the road, any car passing by, and immediately you start looking: maybe the friend has come? The wind on your doors, and suddenly you are alert: maybe he has knocked. . . . Dead leaves in the garden moving hither and thither, and you come out of your home; maybe he has come. . . . Patience is as active as that. It is a waiting. It is not dull, it is very radiant. It is not unconscious; it is not like a stupor. It is like a flame burning bright. One waits. One can wait infinitely, but one waits, expectant, active, alert, watchful.

You cannot force things to happen before their time. The spring will come and the flowers will blossom, but you cannot force the spring. The rain will come, the clouds will cover the sky, the whole thirst of the earth will be gone—but you cannot force it, you have to be patient.

And this is the beauty, that the more patient you are, the quicker is the coming of the spring. If you can be absolutely patient, this very moment spring can come.

Your urgency is creating a trouble for you because it is making you more and more confused, more and more restless, in a hurry. I can understand; the whole Western tradition has taught you only one thing, and that is speed.

Everybody is trying to become rich as quickly as possible, and naturally if you want to be rich quickly you have to find some immoral means—maybe heroin money. All the Western religious leaders are against drugs, but they don't understand that the idea of speed, that everybody has to be fast enough . . . and millions are competing for the same place; naturally there is competition, there is jealousy, there is violence. It does not matter, means don't matter; the end is to reach quickly—either to a powerful position, or to become world famous, or to have all the riches possible.

But trees don't grow impatiently. They move with a grace, with patience, with trust. There is no hurry anywhere else except in your mind. If you really want to be in a state of peace and joy, you will have to unlearn your old habit for achieving things quickly, fast.

Urgency naturally creates the question: "How?" If speed is needed, then the technology is needed. "How" means technology. Meditation is not a by-product of any technology. It does not need any technology. It does not need any "how." It simply needs now.

8 of Rainbows: Ordinariness

The discovered self knows nothing of the abnormal, perverted, neurotic mind.

It becomes simple, it becomes ordinary, but that ordinariness is luminous.

I have heard:

A king and the high priest of the country were both praying early in the morning. It was still dark and they could not see in the temple. The king was saying, "My God, I am just dust under your feet. I am nobody. Have mercy on me!" And the priest said almost the same, maybe in different words but the same thing, "I am nobody. Have mercy on us!"

And then they both heard, with surprise, a third voice. By that time it was becoming a little light and they could see—the poorest beggar of the town was also praying and he was saying, "God, I am dust under your feet. I am nobody. Have mercy on us!"

The king blinked his eyes, turned towards the priest, and said, "Look who is saying that he is just ordinary, that he is nobody. Just look! Who is saying, 'I am nobody'? Just a beggar! The king can say, 'I am nobody,' the high priest can say, 'I am nobody,' but a beggar? How egoistic! How pretentious!"

They both laughed at the idea of the beggar trying to be just like the king or the high priest. He was also bragging about being nobody. The king and the priest thought it insulting. Of course, they can say they are nobody, because everybody knows they are not. Even God knows they are not! They are just being humble. But this poor beggar—what humility is there? He is certainly nobody, and he is saying, "I am nobody." What is the point of saying it?

Remember, your so-called saints have tried to be humble before God, but just in order to be higher in the eyes of people. But my idea of a religious man is that he does not even claim ordinariness—he claims not. He is simply ordinary, whatsoever he is.

A Zen Master, Rinzai, was asked, "What did you do before you were enlightened?"

He said, "I used to chop wood and carry water from the well."

And the man asked, "Now, now that you are enlightened, what do you do?"

He said, "The same thing—chopping wood and carrying water from the well."

The man was puzzled. He said, "I cannot understand. Then what is the difference? Then what is the point of becoming enlightened? Before you used to chop wood and carry water, now you continue the same thing. Then what is the difference?"

And Rinzai laughed. He said, "The difference is: before I was doing it because I *had* to do it, it was a duty. Now it is a joy. The quality has changed—the work is the same."

The small things of life have to be transformed by your inner transformation. This I call the religious quality; everything becomes sacred. Taking a bath, making love, eating food, going to sleep—everything becomes sacred.

❋

Common sense is very rare because to be ordinary . . . the ego prevents you. It wants you to be extraordinary, to be special, to be a

V.V.I.P. It does not allow you to be ordinary, simple, nobody, a nothingness—which is your real nature. In that ordinariness, in that nobodiness, is your real home. Outside it is only misery, suffering, death, anguish, angst. Settling in your simple innocence, knowing nothing . . . just being, and you have become an emperor without any empire. No anxiety of the empire at all, just a pure emperor.

This pure essence of your being is called the buddha, the awakened, the enlightened one. There is no other dance and no other joy. There is no other poetry, there is no other music which can go higher, deeper, which can be without limits, than the joy of an awakened being. It is your birthright.

9 of Rainbows: Ripeness

The only ripeness that is possible is through living.

My whole emphasis is to live the moment whatsoever it is, and live it with tremendous energy.

If you are a young man while young, you will be an old man while old—very wise. You will have known all that is good and bad in life: the day and night, the summer and winter—all you will have known. By your own experience, wisdom will arise. And when you are dying, you will have enjoyed your life so tremendously that you will be able to enjoy your death also.

Only a person who has enjoyed his life becomes capable of enjoying his death. And if you are capable of enjoying your death, you have defeated death. Then there is no more birth for you and no more death for you—you have learned the lesson.

Once I took one of my professors—he was my teacher—I took him to a very beautiful place. Nothing like it exists anywhere in the world. I used to live in Jabalpur, and just thirteen miles away from there flows the beautiful river Narmada. For two miles amidst hills of marble, a two-mile stretch of marble hills . . . it is something not of this world. On a full-moon night it is unbelievable; you cannot believe that it is there. It is so unreal! It has such a hypnotic energy in it.

I took my old professor on a full-moon night, just in the middle of the night when the moon is just overhead. He could not believe that such a beautiful thing is possible on this earth. He said, "What a beautiful place to die!"

But why does this idea arise? "What a beautiful place to live!" would have been absolutely relevant. "What a beautiful place to love! What a beautiful place to dance and sing!" would have been relevant. But the idea arises: "What a beautiful place to die!"

Why this death obsession? Can't you enjoy anything? Can't you delight in anything?

Become aware of such tendencies. And next time when a beautiful moment passes by—dance! sing! paint! love! Death will take care of itself. It will come one day. Be ripe when it comes—and the only ripeness that is possible is through living.

Live deeply, live totally, live wholly, so when death comes and knocks at your door you are ready—ready like a ripe fruit to drop. Just a small breeze comes and the fruit drops; sometimes even without the breeze the fruit drops from its own weight and ripeness. Death should be like that. And the readiness has to come through living.

Everybody seeks, everybody has to seek, but nobody finds by seeking. One day seeking has to be dropped, but when I say "has to be dropped," I simply mean one has to go to the very end of it where it drops of its own accord. That moment is really of great bliss—when there is no seeking, no longing, no desire, nowhere to go, nothing to achieve. One has come home; one has attained relaxation. One is in immense rest . . . not even a ripple in the mind. In that very state god happens.

But that is going to come. Don't be in a hurry. Don't manage it; it is going to come. Seek a little more, and if you want to finish it quickly, run as fast as you can so it will be finished soon. If you go very slowly it can take much time. Right now it will be premature to think to stop it. Let it ripen, and when the fruit is ripe it falls.

10 of Rainbows: We Are the World

WE ARE THE WORLD

Once you understand yourself, you have understood the whole humanity.

In that very understanding a great vision arises in which we are all brothers and sisters and we are all in the same boat.

Why have people become walls? Because walls can be defined. They give you a boundary, a definite shape and form—what Hindus call *nam roop*, name and form.

If you are melting and flowing you don't have boundaries; you don't know where you are and where you end and where the other begins. You go on being together with people so much that all the boundaries by and by become dreamlike. And one day they disappear.

That is how reality is. Reality is unbounded. Where do you think you stop? At your skin? Ordinarily we think, "Of course, we are inside our skins and the skin is our wall, the boundary." But your skin could not be alive if the air was not surrounding it. If your skin is not constantly breathing the oxygen that is being supplied by the surround, your skin cannot be alive. Take away the atmosphere and you will die immediately. Even if your skin has not been scratched you will die. So that cannot be your boundary. There are two hundred miles of atmosphere all around the earth—is that your boundary? That too cannot be your boundary. This oxygen and this atmosphere and the warmth and the life cannot exist without the sun. If the sun ceases to exist or drops dead. . . . One day it is going to happen. Scientists say that in four million years the sun will cool down and drop dead. Then suddenly this atmosphere will not be alive. Immediately you will be dead. So is the sun your boundary?

But now physicists say this sun is connected to some central source of energy which we have not yet been able to find but is suspected— because nothing is unrelated.

So where do we decide where our boundary is? An apple on the tree is not you. Then you eat it, it becomes you. So it is just waiting to become you. It is you potentially. It is your future you. Then you have defecated and you have dropped much rubbish out of the body. Just a moment before, it was you. So where do you decide?

I am breathing. The breath inside me is me, but just a moment before it may have been your breath. It must have been because we are breathing in a common atmosphere. We are all breathing into each other; we are members of each other. You are breathing in me, I am breathing in you.

And it is not only so with breathing, it is exactly so with life. Have you watched? With certain people you feel very alive, they come just bubbling with energy. And something happens in you, a response, and you are also bubbling. And then there are people . . . just their face and one feels one will flop down. Just their presence is enough poison. They must be pouring something into you that is poisonous. And when you come around a person and you become radiant and happy, and suddenly something starts throbbing in your heart, and your heart beats faster, this man must have poured something into you.

We are pouring into each other. We are not separate islands. A cold person becomes like an island and it is a misfortune, it is a great misfortune because you could have become a vast continent and you decided to become an island. You decided to remain poor, when you could have become as rich as you wanted to be.

※

Remember: each human being—maybe the human being is Alexander the Great or just a beggar on the roadside—each human being is as fragile as anybody else. Deep down he is the same—the same consciousness, the same fear, the same death, the same lust, the same love: all exists the same.

Accept yourself, allow your unconscious to be revealed to you. This is how each human being is. By knowing it, you become a different kind of human being. By accepting it, cherishing it, you bring a revolution to your life. And when you look at others with that understanding, you will not find strangers; you will find all are friends.

Everybody is looking for a friend. Everybody is hiding behind a wall and waiting for somebody to say hello, somebody to say, "Why are you there? Come out! I am waiting for you!" . . . somebody to hold hands with. Everybody is waiting for that—somebody to hug, somebody to love and be loved by. . . .

There is nobody who is in any way different from you. Once you understand yourself you have understood the whole humanity. In that very understanding a great vision arises in which we are all brothers and sisters and we are all in the same boat. Then fear disappears; there is nobody to be afraid of. Nervousness disappears; what is there to be nervous about? We are all in the same boat.

※

When thousands and thousands of people around the earth are celebrating, singing, dancing, ecstatic, drunk with the divine, there is no possibility of any global suicide. With such festivity and with such laughter, with such sanity and health, with such naturalness and spontaneity, how can there be a war?

The third world war is not going to happen—I predict it! It is not going to happen, because of you, because of my people around the earth. They are the only hope. Only millions of buddhas are capable of creating the atmosphere for peace, for love, for compassion, for celebration.

Life is not given to you to murder, to destroy. Life has been given to you to create, and to rejoice, and to celebrate.

When you cry and weep, when you are miserable, you are alone. When you celebrate, the whole existence participates with you. Only in celebration do we meet the ultimate, the eternal. Only in celebration do we go beyond the circle of birth and death.

TABLE OF CORRESPONDENCES

	OSHO ZEN TAROT	RIDER-WAITE DECK	CROWLEY DECK
Major Arcana			
O	The Fool	The Fool	The Fool
I	Existence	The Magician	The Magus/Magician
II	Inner Voice	The High Priestess	The Priestess
III	Creativity	The Empress	The Empress
IV	The Rebel	The Emperor	The Emperor
V	No-Thingness	The Hierophant	The Hierophant
VI	The Lovers	The Lovers	The Lovers
VII	Awareness	The Chariot	The Chariot
VIII	Courage	Strength	Adjustment
IX	Aloness	The Hermit	The Hermit
X	Change	Wheel of Fortune	Fortune
XI	Breakthrough	Justice	Lust
XII	New Vision	The Hanged Man	The Hanged Man
XIII	Transformation	Death	Death
XIV	Integration	Temperance	Art
XV	Conditioning	The Devil	The Devil
XVI	Thunderbolt	The Tower	The Tower
XVII	Silence	The Star	The Star
XVIII	Past Lives	The Moon	The Moon
XIX	Innocence	The Sun	The Sun
XX	Beyond Illusion	Judgement	The Aeon
XXI	Completion	The World	The Universe
	The Master	Blank Card	

	OSHO ZEN TAROT	RIDER-WAITE DECK	CROWLEY DECK
Fire/Wands/Wands	**Fire: Mastery of Action**	Wands	Wands
Ace	Ace of Fire–The Source	Ace of Wands	Ace of Wands
2	2 of Fire–Possibilities	II of Wands	II of Wands–Dominion
3	3 of Fire–Experiencing	III of Wands	III of Wands–Virtue
4	4 of Fire–Participation	IV of Wands	IV of Wands–Completion
5	5 of Fire–Totality	V of Wands	V of Wands–Strife
6	6 of Fire–Success	VI of Wands	VI of Wands–Victory
7	7 of Fire–Stress VII of Wands	VII of Wands–Valour	
8	8 of Fire–Traveling	VIII of Wands	VIII of Wands–Swiftness
9	9 of Fire–Exhaustion	IX of Wands	IX of Wands–Strength
10	10 of Fire–Suppression	X of Wands	X of Wands–Oppression
Court Cards			
Page/Princess	Page of Fire–Playfulness	Page of Wands	Princess of Wands
Knight/Prince	Knight of Fire–Intensity	Knight of Wands	Prince of Wands
Queen	Queen of Fire–Sharing	Queen of Wands	Queen of Wands
King	King of Fire–The Creator	King of Wands	Knight of Wands
Water/Cups/Cups	**Water: Mastery of Emotions**	Cups	Cups
Ace	Ace of Water–Going with the Flow	Ace of Cups	Ace of Cups
2	2 of Water–Friendliness	II of Cups	II of Cups–Love
3	3 of Water–Celebration	III of Cups	III of Cups– Abundance
4	4 of Water–Turning In	IV of Cups	IV of Cups–Luxury
5	5 of Water–Clinging to the Past	V of Cups	V of Cups– Dissapointment
6	6 of Water–The Dream	VI of Cups	VI of Cups– Pleasure
7	7 of Water–Projections	VII of Cups	VII of Cups– Debauchery
8	8 of Water–Letting Go	VIII of Cups	VIII of Cups– Indolence
9	9 of Water–Laziness	IX of Cups	IX of Cups– Happiness
10	10 of Water–Harmony	X of Cups	X of Cups–Satiety
Court Cards			
Page/Princess	Page of Water–Understanding	Page of Cups	Princess of Cups
Knight/Prince	Knight of Water–Trust	Knight of Cups	Prince of Cups
Queen	Queen of Water–Receptivity	Queen of Cups	Queen of Cups
King	King of Water–Healing	King of Cups	Knight of Cups

	OSHO ZEN TAROT	RIDER-WAITE DECK	CROWLEY DECK
Clouds/Swords/ Swords	Clouds: Mastery of Mind	Swords	Swords
Ace	Ace of Clouds–Consciousness	Ace of Swords	Ace of Swords
2	2 of Clouds–Schizophrenia	II of Swords	II of Swords–Peace
3	3 of Clouds–Ice-olation	III of Swords	III of Swords– Sorrow
4	4 of Clouds–Postponement	IV of Swords	IV of Swords–Truce
5	5 of Clouds–Comparison	V of Swords	V of Swords–Defeat
6	6 of Clouds–The Burden	VI of Swords	VI of Swords– Science
7	7 of Clouds–Politics	VII of Swords	VII of Swords– Futility
8	8 of Clouds–Guilt	VIII of Swords	VIII of Swords– Interference
9	9 of Clouds–Sorrow	IX of Swords	IX of Swords– Cruelty
10	10 of Clouds–Rebirth	X of Swords	X of Swords–Ruin
Court Cards			
Page/Princess	Page of Clouds–Mind	Page of Swords	Princess of Swords
Knight/Prince	Knight of Clouds–Fighting	Knight of Swords	Prince of Swords
Queen	Queen of Clouds–Morality	Queen of Swords	Queen of Swords
King	King of Clouds–Control	King of Swords	Knight of Swords
Rainbows/ Pentacles/Disks	Rainbows: Mastery of the Physical	Pentacles	Disks
Ace	Ace of Rainbows–Maturity	Ace of Pentacles	Ace of Disks
2	2 of Rainbows– Moment to Moment	II of Pentacles	II of Disks–Change
3	3 of Rainbows–Guidance	III of Pentacles	III of Disks–Works
4	4 of Rainbows–The Miser	IV of Pentacles	IV of Disks–Power
5	5 of Rainbows–The Outsider	V of Pentacles	V of Disks–Worry
6	6 of Rainbows–Compromise	VI of Pentacles	VI of Disks–Success
7	7 of Rainbows–Patience	VII of Pentacles	VII of Disks–Failure
8	8 of Rainbows–Ordinariness	VIII of Pentacles	VIII of Disks–Prudence
9	9 of Rainbows–Ripeness	IX of Pentacles	IX of Disks–Gain
10	10 of Rainbows– We Are the World	X of Pentacles	X of Disks–Wealth
Court Cards			
Page/Princess	Page of Rainbows–Adventure	Page of Pentacles	Princess of Disks
Knight/Prince	Knight of Rainbows– Slowing Down	Knight of Pentacles	Prince of Disks
Queen	Queen of Rainbows–Flowering	Queen of Pentacles	Queen of Disks
King	King of Rainbows–Abundance	King of Pentacles	Knight of Disks

About the Author

Osho's teachings defy categorization, covering everything from the individual quest for meaning to the most urgent social and political issues facing society today. His books are not written but are transcribed from audio and video recordings of extemporaneous talks given to international audiences over a period of 35 years. Osho has been described by the *Sunday Times* in London as one of the "1000 Makers of the 20th Century" and by American author Tom Robbins as "the most dangerous man since Jesus Christ."

About his own work Osho has said that he is helping to create the conditions for the birth of a new kind of human being. He has often characterized this new human being as "Zorba the Buddha"—capable both of enjoying the earthy pleasures of a Zorba the Greek and the silent serenity of a Gautam Buddha. Running like a thread through all aspects of Osho's work is a vision that encompasses both the timeless wisdom of the East and the highest potential of Western science and technology.

Osho is also known for his revolutionary contribution to the science of inner transformation, with an approach to meditation that acknowledges the accelerated pace of contemporary life. His unique "Active Meditations" are designed to first release the accumulated stresses of body and mind, so that it is easier to experience the thought-free and relaxed state of meditation.

Osho Meditation Resort™

The Osho Meditation Resort is a place where people can have a direct personal experience of a new way of living with more alertness, relaxation, and fun. Located about 100 miles southeast of Mumbai in Pune, India, the resort offers a variety of programs to thousands of people who visit each year from more than 100 countries around the world.

Originally developed as a summer retreat for maharajas and wealthy British colonialists, Pune is now a thriving modern city that is home to a number of universities and high-tech industries. The Meditation Resort spreads over 40 acres in a tree-lined suburb known as Koregaon Park. The resort campus provides accommodation for a limited number of guests, and there is a plentiful variety of nearby hotels and private apartments available for stays of a few days or up to several months.

Resort programs are all based in the Osho vision of a qualitatively new kind of human being who is able both to participate creatively in everyday life and to relax into silence and meditation. Most programs take place in modern, air-conditioned facilities and include a variety of individual sessions, courses, and workshops covering everything from creative arts to holistic health treatments, personal transformation and therapy, esoteric sciences, the "Zen" approach to sports and recreation, relationship issues, and significant life transitions for men and women. Individual sessions and group workshops are offered throughout the year, alongside a full daily schedule of meditations.

Outdoor cafes and restaurants within the resort grounds serve both traditional Indian fare and a choice of international dishes, all made with organically grown vegetables from the resort's own farm. The campus has its own private supply of safe, filtered water.

See www.osho.com/resort for more information, including travel tips, course schedules, and guest house bookings.

For more information

about Osho and his work, see:

www.osho.com

a comprehensive Web site in several languages that includes an on-line tour of the Meditation Resort and a calendar of its course offerings, catalogs of books and tapes, a list of Osho information centers worldwide, and selections from Osho's talks.

Or contact:

Osho International

New York

email: oshointernational@oshointernational.com